Cold Noses, Brave Hearts:

Dogs and Men of the 26th Infantry Scout Dog Platoon

Cold Noses, Brave Hearts:

Dogs and Men of the 26th Infantry Scout Dog Platoon

Robert Fickbohm and Sandra Fickbohm Granger

To order additional copies of this book, contact:
Xlibris Corporation
1-888-795-4274
www.Xlibris.com
Orders@Xlibris.com
103239

Contents

Introduction

There must be a reason that a person would write a book about the men and dogs of the 26th Infantry Scout Dog Platoon. I wish this book to be a historical account about the unit, but it's easier to write about my own accounts because I was there. So I will try not to exploit my own stories. The men and dogs of this rather heroic and well-decorated small unit deserve the recognition. During World War II and the Korean War, there was only about a total of 180 men and maybe 90 dogs that served in this small unit. Many people are unaware of the role that dogs have played in saving soldiers' lives, and they are still saving lives today. There have been a number of people in our unit who felt it was necessary to document these accounts but few who had taken action. My grandchildren, along with various nieces and nephews also have encouraged me. But most of all, my daughter, Sandra, took action and deserves credit for all the research, typing and editing that went into it. She kept telling me I needed to write down my stories and eventually, I gave in. In the beginning, I thought it would be easy because I had accumulated quite a bit of historical material, pictures and newspaper articles but I found that sometimes newspaper articles are not so accurate. It also took a lot of sorting, researching facts, and checking with the men involved to try to have an accurate book. It is difficult after so many years to find primary sources, and verify every detail. We wish that we had begun this project many years ago when more of the men of the 26th were still with us. We have tried to compare sources, locate veterans to collaborate with, and collect as much information as we could. Because this unit served wherever they were requested, their records are spread out through many divisions. On any given night, the unit could have been working in two or three different areas along the Main Line of Resistance. These patrols were usually tied to intelligence so names were not given in most reports. Also it seems that many records got dumped at the end of wars as units prepared to go home. Please forgive any errors. We also wish to thank Susan Strange for researching in the Washington, DC area for us. She dug through records at the Military History

Institute at Carlisle, PA, the National Archives, and the Center for Military History at Fort McNair. Her persistence resulted in records finally being declassified as late as January of 2010. There are so many of my buddies who contributed their stories, pictures, and documents, and I wish to thank them. Without their help, this book would never have materialized. If we left any of you out, it was not intentional. As some of you know, many books of military accounts use what I call "military vernacular" or bad language. We hope this book is enjoyed by the children and grandchildren of the men of the 26th and so we have chosen to keep the language relatively clean.

As we researched, we found so many amazing stories of canine courage and intelligence, and met a lot of wonderful, helpful people. There are many other war dog units that deserve recognition, and we enjoyed learning about them, but we have limited this book to those who served with the 26th Infantry Scout Dog Platoon in WWII and Korea. You will find an incomplete roster in Chapter 10. We had to go off of men's memories, partially legible rosters, and slightly burned items from Army Personnel Records. We continue to hope that we will be able to find the members of this unit which we haven't been able to contact.

Robert Fickbohm

Loving Memories of a 26th Infantry Scout Dog Platoon Dog Handler

Like all first meetings it was a little bit tentative.
The first eye contact brought questions to mind.
Would he be up to the unknown task ahead of us;
When told to search the decoy to go out and find.

Weeks of obedience training made us feel better;
Because our respect grew along with confidence.
For this partner that was always so eager to please
For just a few rubs; our task started to make sense.

The lines of this preamble somewhat discloses
A general feeling of experiences most of us felt.
But there is a feeling that is unique to each of us;
For we all knew we had the best dog that was dealt.

They looked to us for love and we responded.
So many dangerous patrols they did dutifully log.
Like the memorial says: "They never complained";
That dog, that dog, that most wonderful dog.

Rest in peace, dear soul buddy.

By Ron McKeown

Chapter One:

Activation and WWII

Our unit was originally formed March 27, 1944 as the 26th Quartermaster War Dog Platoon but was reorganized and re-designated on February 3, 1945 as the 26th Infantry Scout Dog Platoon. The new table of organization and equipment, released in December 1944, changed the name of the Quartermaster units to infantry scout dog platoons and provided that each was to consist of 27 scout dogs. Fifteen Quartermaster War Dog Platoons were activated in World War II. Of these, seven saw service in Europe and eight in the Pacific. During 1945 the Army Ground Forces activated and trained six infantry scout dog platoons. Five of these, however, did not complete their training until V'J Day and consequently were not sent overseas. Thus, all but one of the war dog platoons that saw service in the war were activated and trained by the Quartermaster Corps. (Waller, Anna M. "Dogs and National Defense" Report, 1958)

The first men and dogs to see combat in the Pacific were a small experimental detachment that went over in the later part of 1943. Lt. Robert Johnson was the commander and it seems the men with him were Arthur Tyler, Guy Sheldon, Sgt. Menzo Bowen, Herman Boude, and Sgt. William Jorgensen. They had only eight dogs, two messengers and six scout dogs. The dogs were Duke, Sandy, Lady, Dick, Rocky, Husky, Teddy and Ranger. These eight dogs and the patrols they served were credited with saving countless American lives and eliminating 200 Japanese. These dogs were the first honored by citation certificates issued by the Quartermaster General. This small group successfully proved the value of military dogs. (Wiley, Bonnie. May 7, 1944) Guy Sheldon went on to serve in Korea, and when he found himself in a unit without dogs, he went out and got some dogs from Koreans and formed his own K-9 unit.

In order to become a dog handler in the 26th, soldiers had to volunteer to work with war dogs. This was a relatively new field and still somewhat experimental. Many were men with backgrounds in working with animals but some simply were interested in becoming dog handlers. When describing the type of man needed as dog handlers, 1st Lt. James S. Head, Commanding Officer of the 26th ISDP during WWII, said, "the dog handler must have an appreciation of the value of his work, a high sense of personal responsibility and plenty of initiative in addition to outstanding physical endurance. There are always many situations in which dogs can be used but handlers must be on the alert for these situations. The dogs need handlers who will not wait for situations to come to them but will go look for situations in which the dogs can be used." (Report of 26th QM War Dog Plat. by Lt. Head) The military experimented with dogs as messengers, trackers, mine detectors, pack animals, sentries, sled dogs, rescue dogs, and scouts. These early dogs were mainly donated by the public through the Dogs for Defense Program. During WWII, the greatest demand was for scout dogs.

Training dogs proves to be an art in itself. All military dogs begin with basic obedience; without it, they are worthless. Dogs must respond to both voice and hand signals up to a considerable distance from the trainer. They must be accustomed to small arms fire and artillery as they have such sensitive hearing – three times better than humans. They must learn to go over or through obstacles such as water, foot bridges, ladders, barbed wire, heights, and to ride in vehicles and aircraft. Dogs must then go through more advanced training for their military specialty. They also train for the environment and conditions of the area where they will be utilized. Scout dogs must be trained to be completely silent – a growl or bark at the wrong time will draw enemy fire. This training was conducted at various camps throughout the United States.

Scout dogs are trained to use their scent detecting ability to locate human scent and warn of ambushes. They are used for reconnaissance to determine where the enemy are located, and allow the patrol to gain information about the size of the force and where they will likely attack. The dog's nose can detect humans up to 800 yards away. They also seem to have a sixth sense of danger and will warn handlers of mines, booby traps, incoming mortar, and even snakes. It takes each handler awhile to learn how to utilize a dog's special abilities, and to learn how his dog communicates an alert.

In July of 1944, a Mobilization Training Program for Dog handlers was issued by the War Department. It laid out the training needed before men and dogs entered combat. All handlers finished basic training before being transferred to a dog training center. All needed to pass weapon handling courses. They then completed Basic Technical Training which varied somewhat based on the type of dog to be handled. Subjects required of scout and messenger dog handlers included: Army Orientation, Basic Military Subjects, Knots and Lashings, Rules of Land Warfare, Village Fighting, Cover and Movement, Map and Aerial Photo Reading, Patrol Operations, and Specific training for the use of the dog. This portion of training was 112 hours of classes. Then they had to learn Basic Dog Training and Handling, Diseases of Dogs, Feeding, First Aid, Grooming, Kennel Care, Orientation to War Dogs, Parasites, Principles of Dog Training, Processing, Psychology, Transportation, and Specialized Dog Training and Handling for another 672 hours of class. Then they had to work with their own dogs and establish rapport. They had to learn how their individual dog alerted, how to perform night operations, and then train together with their unit for 144 hours. (Mobilization Training Program, No. 10-5)

The men and dogs of the 26th Infantry Scout Dog Platoon of WWII came together at the "War Dog Training Center" at Camp San Carlos which was located in the foothills above the city of San Carlos, CA. Bill Garbo of the 26th ISDP describes how it looked when he arrived in the fall of 1943. "The camp was small, only six barracks, a classroom building, kitchen, the headquarters building, a K9 kitchen, drill field and a building called the Devonshire Club. The dog kennel area was spread out over several hills. Each dog had a wooden kennel box with straw bedding inside. There were approximately 500 dogs and 300 men at the camp."

Bill Garbo (left) and Ray Smith (right) at Camp San Carlos in 1943.
Picture from Bill Garbo

Over a three month period, each soldier trained as many as six dogs for scout, rescue, guard and messenger duties. Before graduation, they were required to demonstrate the dogs' skills for the officers. The dogs had to follow a given sequence of silent signals. Spectators were always impressed with these demonstrations. Before going overseas, the dogs had to pass a physical examination and photos were taken of the dogs and handlers.

The 26th War Dog Platoon left Camp San Carlos on Mother's Day, May 14, 1944. We had our "dogs in two army trucks, with the canvas lashed down so that no one could see the cargo inside as we passed through the cities in route to The Presidio in San Francisco army base where Fort Mason is located, on the edge of the Bay. The Liberty ship (Irving M. Scott) was tied up at the pier waiting for us."

Lt. Head on board the ship
Photo from George Diller

"I boarded the ship with 30 men in the 26th War Dog Platoon, led by Lt. Head, to Fort Morgan in San Francisco for the trip overseas. It had been specially prepared to take the 26th War Dog platoon. Special wooden shelters had been built and lashed to the deck just aft of mid-ship to house our 60 dogs. Our sleeping quarters were to be two wooden structures built and lashed to the upper deck to house 30 men of the platoon while Lt. Head and Sgt. Robertson were housed within the ship near the captain's quarters.

I checked my watch; we sailed under the Golden Gate Bridge at 10 minutes after 2:00 PM; my last view of the USA. It did not occur to me that this might be the last time I would see the United States of America. Fog and rough water engulfed our liberty ship just outside the Golden Gate Bridge; before sun-down I was seasick with many others aboard. It lasted three days. And then calm seas prevailed and I could eat a meal without throwing up. We were all alone for 31 days before reaching Milne Bay, New Guinea June 15th, 1944." (Garbo, William "Memoirs")

They were guided through nets and mines protecting the bay by an Australian Sub Chaser. After a short stay, men and dogs boarded an overloaded C47. They definitely needed the entire runway. Their destination was Aitape, Papua, New Guinea. They set up camp with 4 squad tents placed in a circle in a jungle clearing within a few yards of the beach.

General view of the dog's rest area near Aitape, August 3, 1944
photographer Sgt. Carl Wienke (from National Archives)

The 26th was commanded by 1st Lt. James S. Head of Carlyle, Illinois. He was well qualified by prior work with guide dogs and hunting falcons. The other dog handlers were all first rate. They had a strong belief in dogs and what they could accomplish. 1st Lt. Head wrote a letter July 5, 1944 in which he said, "The unit as a whole feels privileged to be the one operating in this particular theatre because of where we think our operations may be in the future." (Head, 1st Lt. James, 7/5/1944) They arrived in the Pacific to jungle growth that was so heavy that you could not see a man unless he was moving. This was a difficult and uncomfortable feeling for soldiers, but the presence of a scout dog was helpful. The handheld walkie-talkies were not reliable even over a short distance in the damp and dense jungle. Messenger dogs would soon prove their usefulness in communication. The 26th first went into combat on Biak Island on July 1, 1944. It was attached to the 41st Division on Biak, and with the 32nd and 31st Divisions on Aitape. They made the assault landing on Morotai Island with the 31st Division. Its handlers and dogs were split up among the 42nd, 25th, 6th, and 32nd Divisions when they hit the beach of Lingayan Gulf on the island of Luzon in the Philippines. They also participated in the occupation of Japan. The platoon was in continuous combat from July of 1944 until its relief in the late fall of 1945.

Aug. 7, 1944: John Gatto removes message from the dog,
and delivers it to 1st Lt. James Head on Aitape.
Photographer: Sgt Carl Wienke, (National Archives)

Whenever they were first attached to a unit, they found opposition. The handlers and the officers all came from the Quartermaster branch and had not trained much with the ground forces. Some of them were not in combat ready physical condition. "Infantryman tended to distrust anyone with a QM patch on his sleeve. After all, the responsibility of the Quartermaster Corps was to supply the material to support combat troops, not to actually participate in the fighting." (Lemish, Michael G. War Dogs, 1996) This may be the reason the platoons became the responsibility of the ground forces, and the Quartermaster Corps only retained responsibility for supplying dogs. In addition, the soldiers were unaware of the value of dogs. They felt they would be a nuisance at best, and at worst, they might get men killed if they barked and drew the attention of the enemy.

The 26th demonstrated their dogs' skills, explained their usefulness and basically begged for the opportunity to do what they had been trained for. Soldiers came to appreciate the advance warning the dogs gave since the Japanese came in at night as well as during the day when you least expected it. They soon were glad to see war dogs and gained comfort from their presence.

Patrols were dispatched every day to confirm enemy movement, evaluate his strength and control the perimeter. Not just the members of the patrol gained comfort from knowing the dogs were on the job, the handlers slept better too. The men of the 26th had a constant companion and friend. Their Supreme Allied Commander, General Dwight D. Eisenhower, put it like this "The friendship of a dog is precious. It becomes even more so when one is so far removed from home . . . he is the 'one person' to whom I can talk without the conversation coming back to the war." (Gray, Ernest, <u>Dogs of War</u>)

Lt. Head, E. Smith with dog Fearless, R. Aldred and Skipper, G. Bertram with Loopy, R. Smith and Rex, L. Long and Silver, and A. Lush with Marc on Anaho Trail near Aitape, New Guinea. (National Archives)

Members of the 26th canine platoon served all of the combat units dug in along the Driniumor River. Bill Garbo tells more of his experience here. "Teddy was with me at all times. I was assigned to make patrols with one infantry outfit that had built elaborate foxholes with coconut tree logs over them; dirt was piled on top of the logs to provide protection from artillery and mortar fire. Another trooper, my dog Teddy, and I were in a covered foxhole on one extremely dark night; when my dog Teddy never barked but he let me know someone was out there by nudging me vigorously with his head. A Jap crawled up and threw a bundle (Satchel charge) of dynamite into our foxhole. We lobbed hand grenades and took cover as the dynamite cap went off but the satchel charge did not explode because it was wet. I was deaf for a while and my ears were ringing from the loud explosion of the cap. It was a long miserable night; our foxhole buddies around us didn't know whether we were dead or alive until morning; they were surprised and happy when we crawled out of our hole with gun powder all over us. After a bath in the river we looked normal again, if possible under the circumstances.

I took Teddy on many patrols; he successfully carried messages back to the CP (Command Post). Once Teddy had to cross the river after a heavy rain shower; the muddy water had risen and carried him downstream out of sight. He came running back to the CP muddy and wringing wet after finally swimming across somewhere downstream. The message he carried was vital to the intelligence regarding the enemy buildup and subsequent attack. I got the details about Teddy going downstream when I returned with the patrol before sundown." (Garbo, William "Memoirs") Teddy's arrival had been in time to lay artillery into a large concentration of Japanese troops.

George Diller, Teddy, and William Garbo at Milne Bay
Photo compliments of Bill Garbo

"The fighting on Morotai in the Netherlands East Indies illustrates the manner in which scout dogs could be used to maximum benefit. There the enemy offered at first but slight resistance, retreating into the mountainous jungles of the interior and then sallying forth in small groups to harass the Americans. In patrol operations designed to uncover Japanese bivouac areas, supply dumps, and line of communications the 26th War Dog Platoon proved invaluable. During the period 17 September – 10 November 1944, the dogs made more than one hundred patrols with infantry troops ranging from a patrol of five men to a rifle company of two hundred or more. The Commander of the 155th Infantry Regiment reported that the dogs never failed to alert at less than 75 yards and not a single casualty was suffered while a scout dog was being employed. The ability of the dog to pick up enemy bivouacs, positions, patrols, troop reconnaissance, etc. long before our patrol reached them frequently enabled our troops to achieve surprise and inflict heavy casualties on the Japanese." (Waller, Anna, "Dogs and National Defense")

L-R: Jack Sullivan, Chester Lacey, Edwin Smith, Ellis Tucker,
and T/Sgt.Robert Robertson on Morotai Island 1944
Photo compliments of George Diller

There are many stories of the way that scout dogs and messenger dogs aided the soldiers in the Pacific Theater. We have tried to verify the accuracy of the accounts but it is difficult when so few of the soldiers can be interviewed. Some of the names of men and dogs may be listed incorrectly, but the incidents are true. On Morotai, "Robert K. Robertson and his dog King were preceding a combat patrol along a well-worn path, when King alerted so strongly that Robertson knew the enemy must be nearby and advised the patrol leader to deploy his men off the path they were following. He and his dog made a slow cautious advance and had not gone far when they discovered that they had almost walked into a well prepared trap along the banks of a river which the patrol was soon to cross. Noise made by the troops, however, gave their presence away and the Japs opened up everything from knee mortars and machine guns, but the infantrymen, having taken heed of Robertson's warning, had taken cover and were able to withdraw without losing a man." (Southtown Economist, Chicago, IL 1/3/1945)

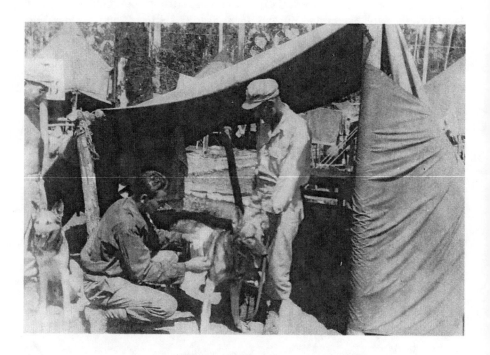

The Vet Tent on Morotai Island
Milton Leavitt, Jack Sullivan (vet) and Herman Schut
Photo from George Diller

"As King (#2) and his handler, T-5 Walter Cranford, were leading a patrol in a steep climb up a ridge, King alerted and plunged abruptly. Because of poor footing, Crawford was jerked from his feet and lost his hold on King's leash. As the handler fell, a rifle bullet creased his shoulder. King dashed forward with a rasping growl. Out of a foxhole to the fore, a Jap rifleman popped like a rabbit. He took one terrified look at the charging K-9, threw away his rifle and ran for his life. Thereupon King whirled and charged across in another direction. A second Jap rifleman gave a repeat performance. King was all for catching him, but at Cranford's call the dog obediently returned to his wounded master." (Downey, Fairfax, <u>Dogs For Defense</u>)

Diller, Cranford, and Sullivan
Picture from George Diller

"Vividly Captain Head remembers a hot, all-night fight when the patrol, which had penetrated for some distance into hostile territory, was discovered and jumped by the enemy. The Nips launched one furious attack after another. First they would lay down a mortar barrage on the American patrol's position, fling a shower of grenades, and then charge with fixed bayonets. The Americans, to avoid disclosing their positions, fired only enough to break the bayonet charges. Sgt. Glen Ormson with his dog "Bruce," and T-5 Roy Long with his dog "Silver," were sharing a foxhole. A Jap grenade plunked squarely into it. Ormson grabbed for it to throw it out, but it slipped from his fingers, rolled under "Silver" and exploded with an ear-splitting bang. The poor dog was blown to bits but his body, by absorbing the force of the explosion, undoubtedly had saved the lives of the two men and the second dog. Both Long and Ormson, severely wounded by multiple fragments, lay dazed with shock and pain. They looked up to see two Japs on the rim of their foxhole, bayonets poised for the thrust. Helplessly and hopelessly, the American soldiers lay there. It was then that the dog "Bruce" sprang up with a full-throated roar. The Japs dropped their rifles and ran." (Downey, Fairfax, Dogs for Defense)

George Diller and "Duke" taken at Milne Bay in 1944
Photo from George Diller

Duke was a messenger dog. He saved George Diller's life before they even left American soil. They were still training at Camp San Carlos. "I had him on a leash and we were walking along the side of the hill. I didn't even know there was a snake. Duke made a dive, I let go of the leash, and Duke got a hold of that rattlesnake and finished him off with a couple of shakes." George and Ellis Tucker would send Duke back and forth between them with important information. George says that he was carrying a message back from a patrol on Morotai Island in 1944 and never made it back. After losing Duke, he worked with William Jackson and they had a trail dog named Vicky. She was a Labrador.

Members of the 26th exit the USS Mercury at Luzon.
Photo from George Diller

The 26th participated in the landing on Luzon. That was January 9, 1945. As they waded ashore, they were shelled by Japanese mountain guns. George says no one in the 26th was hit. He was working Wolf, a scout dog, as they moved inland. They were attached to the 25th Division and went to Balete Pass. That was some of the heaviest fighting the 26th participated in. The dogs led many patrols around that Pass.

Between "24 January 1945 and 7 April 1945, all of the dogs were employed continuously. The only trouble encountered was a seriously inadequate number of dogs. Consequently, many units that desired to use dogs were not able to obtain them. In many instances even when dogs were available, it was not possible to get them to the place where they were needed in time. A sufficient number of dogs is essential in order to have them immediately available when needed. 7 April 1945, due to a high percentage of combat losses, the platoon reverted to Division control to be used only on special missions. (Head, Lt. James. Historical Report, July 18, 1945)

One dog, Skippy, "led a patrol which halted for the night deep in enemy territory and dug foxholes. Skippy and his handler, Sgt. Rocky Oliver, bedded down in theirs with the dog tied short to his master's wrist and sank into a sound sleep. In the middle of the night the leash's jerking woke the sergeant. He felt for his dog. Skippy was on his feet and tense. Oliver climbed out of the foxhole and crept over to the guard. No one could discern anything suspicious in the darkness, but Skippy continued to show keen interest in a particular direction. Oliver pointed and advised an automatic rifle burst. The B.A.R. man let it go. Immediately afterward, Skippy relaxed and returned to his foxhole to resume his interrupted slumber. Next morning investigation disclosed three freshly-killed Japs." (Downey, Fairfax. Dogs for Defense)

Cpl. Frank Oliver and "Skippy" close to Balete Pass, Luzon
Photo by Winston (National Archives)

Here is a newspaper story about Cpl. Oliver and his war dog. "In a surgical ward of an American Army field hospital attached to the 25th Division, you will find in adjoining beds Cpl. Frank R Oliver and Skipper of the War Dog Platoon. Oliver has shrapnel in a leg, arm and shoulder while Skipper has a bullet wound through his lower jaw. The war dog was trained to be suspicious of strangers and hospital attendants could do nothing with him until they moved his master, Corporal Oliver into the next bed. Oliver made Skipper submit to ministrations. Both are well on road to recovery. They were wounded leading an advance patrol in the Caraballo Mountains of east-central Luzon." (Galveston Daily News, Galveston, TX 4/16/1945)

Ellis Tucker, Ed Smith, and Walter Skillings with unidentified dogs
Photo from George Diller

By June 17, 1945, the platoon was attached to the 63rd Infantry even though only 25% of the unit was in effective combat condition. June 22, 1945 the 26th ISDP was on a patrol. There were slight showers. A G-3 Operations report gives brief details of a night battle that involved several companies. Their supporting weapons had been held up due to landslides along the trail. Friendly planes strafed forward positions and resulted in one man being killed in action and seven more wounded. The fighting was fierce. A Japanese ambush of a supply line resulted in another man being killed in action and eight wounded. While trying to retake a position held by gorillas, a patrol operating with scout dogs encountered an unknown number of Japanese. They suffered one KIA and one WIA. They captured three enemy soldiers but a scout dog was killed during the action. I have been unable to find a veteran who can identify that dog. (G-3 Operations Report dated 22 June 1945) Apparently both Lt. Head and Sgt. Schut were wounded on this night because they were awarded purple hearts.

In another incident, the silent scout dog, Mark, gave an alert to his handler, Sgt. David M. Williams, which warned the patrol of the presence of enemy soldiers in the vicinity. They were leading an infantry patrol of men from the 25th Division through the Caraballo Mountains on northern Luzon. This led to the killing of three Japanese soldiers. The 26th Infantry Scout Dog Platoon have led hundreds of patrols during their 165 consecutive days of combat on Luzon. (Carroll Daily Times, 8/3/1945)

Sgt. David M. Williams with scout dog, Mark on June 23, 1945
Photo sent by Lt. Head to Public Relations Officer of 25th Inf. (National Archives)

The 26th was part of the occupying force in Japan from around October 26, 1945 until January 31, 1946. Sonny Moore, who was assigned to the 26th ISDP on May 26th, 1945, tells about being in Japan. "We went into Nagoya on an LST. We were the first overseas combat troops to land there. We went in with loaded rifles, still scared, and didn't know what to expect. I rode on a self-propelled 105mm cannon with my Scout Dog, Captain – I called him Cap for short. It was around eight in the morning when we landed and a lot of people were walking around with their backs turned to us – it made us all very nervous. We learned later that by turning their backs to us it meant respect. We thanked God for that . . . . It was an interesting experience, to say the least. The Battalion took over a Military School about

2 miles east of Komaki. Finally, after about 15 months in combat, we (the unit) had a wooden roof over our heads and wooden floors to walk on – it was heaven. No more mud, rain, bugs, rats, and the rest of that stuff we endured in combat. I will always remember my good buddy, Bert Cohen saying, "Sonny, here we are in Japan—a short while ago we were shootin' at 'em and now we're kissing 'em." Soon orders came down from Headquarters in Nagoya that all Scout Dog men were relieved of all duties except caring for their dogs. That was good news; we all needed a rest, especially the dog teams. There were only farms around our camp and the people were afraid of us. We only saw little kids, old men and women at first as they had been told American soldiers would violate them. Later on we were shown cartoons in the newspaper that were published in Japan during the war, showing what the Japanese people could expect from the Americans if and when we invaded Japan. Cap and I got to know a number of farmers and their families after a few weeks. I spent many a cold night with my hands under a blanket over the little charcoal bowl, learning Japanese and teaching my Japanese friends English. The young women slowly began 'coming out of the woods' after a while, and we all began to appreciate being alive and creating new friendships. Yes, those were the happiest days of my military career. I went to Nagoya as a Corporal and came back a Tech Sergeant. We came home on a Liberty ship to Seattle in February 1946." The 26th ISDP was inactivated on February 16, 1946 at Fort Lawton, Washington.

Sonny Moore and Captain
Photo from Sonny Moore

The 26th definitely earned the honors it received. George Diller kept track of just the Japanese air raids the 26th survived when he was with it – 159! Its members were awarded one Silver Star, eight Bronze Stars, and seven Purple Hearts (two with oak leaf clusters) for wounds in action. None of the men were killed in action. All members were awarded the prized Combat Infantryman Badge. They were awarded the Philippine Presidential Unit Citation for participation in the war against the Japanese Empire during the period Oct. 17, 1944 to July 4, 1945. The platoon was given a unit citation from the 31st division and one from the 6th Division.

Walter J. Hanna, Infantry Commanding Officer wrote the following to the members of the 26th concerning their commendation:

"1. On behalf of every Officer and enlisted man of this organization, I wish to express our appreciation of the excellent work you have done. During your attachment to the Infantry, your performance of duty has been outstanding.
2. To those of you who accompanied some 200 of our patrols, I am especially grateful. Your courage, aggressiveness, endurance and devotion to duty has earned you the respect and admiration of every man in the regiment. I also wish to thank your platoon leader and platoon sergeant for their fine cooperation and technical assistance.
3. It was a pleasure to have you and your splendid dogs with us. It is my earnest wish that I may enjoy the opportunity of having you with us again in the future. You carry with you the sincere best wishes of every member of this organization for good luck and good fortune in all your future work." (Hanna, Walter, 22 December, 1944)

The 31st, 25th, and 6th Divisions all requested that the 26th ISDP be permanently assigned to them. Perhaps the greatest sign of their effectiveness was the fact that in the final months of the war, the Japanese made an intense effort to kill the dogs of the 26th. They would concentrate fire on the dog and handler because they knew what a useful weapon they were for the United States Army.

Russell Thompson holds his attacking dog back
(National Archives)

Proof that the 26th performed well the job they had begged to do comes from letters of appreciation and support sent by those who were served by the dogs and handlers. 1st Lt. Louis J. Haahp, Infantry, wrote "My experience with the dogs has proven them to be of very great help in locating ambushes or areas recently occupied by Japs. On one occasion, I was a member of a patrol ambushed late one afternoon. We returned the next day and when we had approached the general area of the ambush, the dog alerted us. A group of six Japs was located a short distance from their position of the night before and were killed without loss to our patrol. The conduct of the dog-man has in every case been one of example to the other members of the patrols." (Haahp, Louis. 26 November, 1944)

The 26th Infantry Scout Dog Platoon along with other war dog units proved the value of using dogs in the military. Lt. Col. Peter Calza felt that we needed more platoons. "The two infantry scout dog platoons (25th ISDP and 26th ISDP) operating under I Corps have been most helpful in locating well concealed Japanese positions and preventing night surprise infiltration attacks. It is believed each division operating in mountainous or jungle terrain should have a minimum of one scout dog platoon attached; two platoons could be usefully employed in dense terrain." (Calza, Peter, 18 April, 1945) These reports caused the War Department to authorize scout dog platoons in the postwar Military Establishment. For the first time in its history, the Army recognized that dogs possessed sufficient tactical value to justify their inclusion among the regular peacetime units.

"At the end of the war, The Quartermaster Corps put into operation a plan for return of war dogs to their civilian owners. Dogs were sent to a reprocessing section for rehabilitation to civilian life. Dogs were trained that every human is friendly. They were tested for such things as reaction to people riding around them on bicycles or placed in an area with a great amount of noise. Before return, each dog was given a final check by a veterinary officer. The government paid for the shipment of the dog to the owner. Those dogs unwanted by the original owners were sold to the public by the Treasury Department, with the assistance of Dogs for Defense. It took more than two years to return all borrowed dogs." (Boon, Major Kevin, 1998)

Those dogs fortunate enough to have survived the war, were returned to the United States. Fort Robinson was a dog rehabilitation center and prepared the dogs for return to civilian life. 95% of the dogs were to be returned to their original owners. Many dog handlers wrote to the owner of their dog and asked if they could adopt the dog. After they explained how much they loved the dog and what the two of them had endured together, many dog owners were willing to give the dog to his former handler. Sonny Moore had handled the dog, Captain, in the Pacific theater. Sonny had grown up training animals for a family variety show that performed around the country. Captain was a very intelligent animal and apparently Sonny, and others, had taught him some extracurricular activities. For a news reporter on the front lines, Lt. Head had demonstrated one of Captain's skills. Captain lay under Head's cot. Head threw a smoking cigarette on the floor and quietly said, "Captain". The war dog emerged and Head told him to put it out. Captain looked around for the smoking butt, walked over and put a paw on it, and the deed was done. (The Brownsville Herald, 6-8-1945) Sonny Moore was with the dogs when they came back to the United States. When Sonny was discharged, he had to see his scout dog, Captain, return to his original owners. In an unusual twist, the dog so grieved for his master that he wouldn't eat. The owner, through a radio and newspaper search, found Sonny and sent Captain to him. Captain joined the "Sonny Moore and his Roustabouts" show and was a key performer until he died in 1953.

Captain Joins Sonny and His Roustabouts
Photo from Sonny Moore

Dogs who were not able to be returned to owners, were offered up for adoption. Requests for the veteran war dogs were sent to Dogs for Defense. Each request was investigated to be sure that the prospective purchaser was in a position to offer a good home. They were charged a minimum cost and had to pay shipping from Fort Robinson. According to Lt. General Edmund B. Gregory, the quartermaster general, "the public may rest assured no dog will be released from army custody until every effort has been made to insure its return to civilian life under the most auspicious possible circumstances." ("Nebraska Army Post Trains All War Dogs", The Nebraska State Journal, June 17, 1945.) Each recipient of a veteran war dog received information on the care and handling of the dog, a list of the basic commands it knew, and a war dog training manual.

One woman wrote to the army, "Our dog has benefited by his year in the army and since his return, has been as gentle and friendly and loving as before . . . . . Many people were under the impression that he would be a vicious animal on his return, but that is definitely not so. We are very proud of our returned veteran." (Sanderson, Jeannette, War Dog Heroes)

While only 5% of veteran dogs had no owner to return to, Dogs for Defense received thousands of requests to adopt them. They gave preference to World War II veterans and the owners of dogs who had died in the service. These former war dogs were almost always successful citizens in their peace time existence. Of all the war dogs returned to civilian life, only four had to be returned for more training. One family, Major and Mrs. V.E. Reemes, had this to say about the dog that they adopted. "Fritz was not our dog when he was entered in Dogs For Defense. Therefore, we are not able to compare the change, if any, in the dog now and prior to his Army training. As his new owners, we are most satisfied. He is very affectionate, gentle with every member of the family, courteous to strangers, not antagonistic toward men making deliveries to the home, as newsboy, garbage or milk men. He is friendly with the other dogs in the neighborhood. In fact, having him has been nothing but a pleasure. He has no objectionable habits at all. We are most grateful to the organization of Dogs For Defense and the patient men who trained these dogs; and for the opportunity to own one of these splendid animals!" (Pfaffenberger, Clarence and Finnegan, George, Paper)

Chapter Two:

Between Wars

The end of WWII was just the beginning for the 26th Infantry Scout Dog Platoon. The success of these teams meant that the military would utilize dogs more in the future. After WWII, the Army determined that dogs used for pack and sled service, mine detection, and messengers were no longer needed because of advances in technology. Sentry dogs remained important in guarding installations to prevent thievery and saving the Army millions of dollars. The scout dogs had demonstrated the ability to save lives by giving our soldiers warning of enemy positions. In 1946, the Army decided to purchase its dogs rather than ask for donations from the public. They would be able to keep the dogs after investing in their training, and not have to return them to their previous owners after their tour of duty. The German Shepherd was chosen as the dog most suitable for these duties because of its temperament, intelligence and endurance. By war's end, the K-9 Corps had dwindled to six platoons, one of which was the 26th Infantry Scout Dog Platoon. After returning to the states, all but the 26th had been disbanded. Actually, the 26th had been inactivated at Fort Lawton, Washington in February 1946 but a few of its dogs and men still had some time left to serve in the army. Men from several different units ended up in Fort Riley, Kansas where the unit was reactivated on August 1, 1946. During this time period, dog training in the United States became centered in Fort Riley.

While at Fort Riley, the dogs were mostly used for demonstration purposes. Teams gave demonstrations around the United States, appeared on television shows, and accompanied infantry units on maneuvers. Some of these even went up into Canada. A newspaper clipping from Fort Riley says, "Sgt. William S. Layher left the ground general school center here the past week for Ottawa, Canada with the 26th Infantry Scout Dog Platoon. Along with nine other men of the platoon, he was to exhibit his scout dog, 'Pal', at the National Sportsmen Show of Canada." (Centralia Washington Newspaper April 24, 1947) Sgt. Ralph D. Nelson, with his dog Wolf, was also part of the team that appeared in Canada. (The Progress, Clearfield, PA April 25, 1947) Sgt. Nelson went on to serve as a sentry dog handler in Okinawa in 1950.

Leonard "Buck" Ferrell with his dog, Duchess, was one of those men that served between wars. He says that the most enjoyable time he spent in the military was with the 26th ISDP. He was sent to Camp Carson, CO in November or December 1949, and after basic K-9 training, worked with dogs in the 10th Mountain Division. He was part of the group who got to enjoy the winter in Alaska with the dogs during December through April. He says that Duchess taught him a lot that helped him survive in Korea. The Army convinced him to re-enlist in 1950 so that he could go to Germany with scout dogs, but then transferred him to the 2nd Infantry Division. He served with distinction, earning a Silver Star and Purple Heart, but always regretted not being able to continue with the men and dogs of the 26th.

Buck Ferrell and Duchess, 1949
Photo from Buck Ferrell

Buck Ferrell remembered some of those first men and dogs that went to Korea. Buck says, "I remember William J. Irving and dog Jon. It is good to know Jon finally got someone to handle him. He was a good dog. He also was a friend. He was next to the front gate at Camp Forsythe. I fed him and cleaned up his kennel. He was a great dog."

Jon refuses a handful of hamburger until given permission to eat by his handler.
US Army Photo by Cpl Mervyn Lew (National Archives)

One man who deserves a lot of credit for service to war dogs is Ralph Trickey. He devoted many years to war dogs and the military in general. He got drafted in 1943 and volunteered for the K-9 Corp after Basic training. He was sent to Fort Robinson and was impressed by that fort's heritage, brick buildings, and the way he was treated. His first 2 weeks was spent pulling Company Details and Kennel Care. He truly believed "it was a well thought out way to begin your K-9 training". Eventually he was assigned to the Instructor's Group and was exposed to sentry, messenger, casualty, scout, trail and mine dogs. Trickey then went with the 39th Quartermaster War Dog Platoon to the Pacific. The 39th's exploits deserve another whole book. They received a citation from the 33rd Division which reads in part: "More than 200 combat patrols during the period from 9 March to 23 May, 1945 . . . More than 200 known enemy killed by patrols after advancing into areas alerted by dogs . . . . Any number of times parties were saved from ambush by the alertness of the dogs and their handlers." (Fairfax Downey, Dogs for Defense)

When Trickey got back to the states, he was released from the service so he collected his war dog "Terry" and entered civilian life. Terry remained with him until his death in December of 1953. He was 12 years old.

Ralph Trickey with Terry
Photo from his daughter-in-law, Christine Trickey

He found something lacking and missed war dogs so he re-enlisted in the army. He ended up back at Fort Robinson, then moved on to the 26th Infantry Scout Dog Platoon at Fort Riley, KS. He trained a lot of dogs and handlers and did demonstrations all over the United States, even appearing on a TV program in Chicago.

Hans, casualty dog, 26th ISDP, is harnessed by Sgt. RalphTrickey
Photograph by Cpl. Charles Adamson, Ft. Riley, KS (National Archives)

He tells about developing the unit prior to the Korean War. "We started receiving German Shepherds for the Quartermaster. Most of the dogs passed their physical and gun shyness test. The Korean War had begun and our unit was alerted for a Korean Assignment. More shepherds were received and to bring our unit up to strength, our Commander interviewed recruits that had completed their basic training with the 10th Infantry Division at Camp Function, KS. Our commander, Lt. Dean, was very successful in obtaining the best recruits for dog handlers. Our unit was ordered to send an advance squad to Korea and the full unit would follow in about 60 days, as the recruits would have completed their dog handler course. For some reason, some of our dogs were not received as requested and we had to delay our departure to Korea. The advance squad was in Korea and doing an excellent job. A Cpl.

had been put in charge of the unit, and did a good job informing commanders of the proper utilization of Scout Dogs."

The man in charge of that advance group was William J. Irving. He had participated during WWII as a member of the War Dog Platoon that had been stationed in the China-Burma-India Theater. That group distinguished itself in battle and should have its own book too. Not many of those men are left to tell the story but I believe that others from CBI went on to serve with war dogs in the Korean War or to train those who came after them.

MEMBERS of CBI War Dog Detachment shown here include:
Top row, left to right: Weston, Gessler, Balak, Misner, Clarke, Raemer.
Bottom row: Erdman, Gross, Armstrong, Irving and Cowan.
Photo near Myitkyina, after the unit had cleared out a Japanese pillbox.
Photo from Dick Zika

Chapter Three:

Korean War Begins

How did we end up in Korea? Korea was a small peninsula with a ridge of mountains running from the Yaber River in the north to Pusan in the south. The west coast area was flat with wide muddy river plains. Much of the rest of the land had endless hills which become high, rough mountains with steep valleys. The population was poor and survived on sustenance farming. To the rest of the world, Korea was an insignificant country lacking in natural beauty. It had harsh winters, hot humid summers, and a monsoon season that turned the poor roads into mud holes.

Area around Kumwha where the 26th ISDP spent a lot of time
Photo courtesy of Charles Hunt

Why then did this small country become the center of a bitter war? Korea, like Poland, stood in the path of imperialistic nations. It had struggled as a Japanese colony, and at the end of World War II became divided by the United States and the Soviet Union as a way to accept the surrender of those Japanese in residence. They divided the country at the 38th parallel with the Russians accepting the surrender of those to the north and the United States accepting surrenders to the south. Abruptly the Soviets stopped any movement across the 38th parallel, and Korea found itself divided into two nations, a communist North and a democratic south. While the United States prepared South Korea to become an independent nation, the USSR began to train and arm the North Korean People's Army. They had become a satellite country for Russia.

Backed by the Soviet Union, the North Koreans decided to attack South Korea and re-unify the country. They felt the United States would not want to commit to war. On June 24, 1950 at four in the morning, 89,000 North Koreans stormed across the 38th parallel with Russian tanks, artillery and a small air force. The South Koreans were poorly equipped and faced this onslaught with 65,000 troops. The North Koreans swept down through South Korea.

Our state department received a report of the attack from Ambassador Muccio at 9:20 PM on June 25, 1950. The United Security Council passed a resolution calling for the immediate cessation of hostilities and for North Korean forces to withdraw. President Truman and the State Department agree to provide assistance to the South Koreans. The United States had become involved in the Korean War. (Summers, Harry G. Jr. Korean War Almanac)

During this time period, at least two people played a key role in determining how the 26th Infantry Scout Dog Platoon came to be in Korea. Madame Rosenberg was the Assistant Secretary of Defense for Manpower. After one of her trips to the war zone in Korea, she directed Lt. Colonel George Ish to "determine the degree of savings in manpower and funds that can be affected by maximum utilization of dogs in the performance of scouting and patrolling in zones of combat, and in the performance of physical security missions and guarding critical installations." (Ish, Lt. Col George, Jan. 1996) The first step was to determine what needs for dogs existed in each of the armed services. One of the first major needs to surface was for scout dogs in Korea. Dogs were mostly being trained at Fort Riley, Kansas.

L-R: Going over jumps are Duchess with handler, Edwin H. Bristol, Orrin with John C. Chappelear, and Barrie with Huda L. Green at Fort Riley. Photographer: Cpl. Charles Adamson (National Archives)

Pfc. Virgil E. Price, receives a message from Chipper after he slides to a stop. Photo by Cpl. Charles Adamson, Ft. Riley (National Archives)

Because of the urgent need for scout dogs, seven men and dogs (all that were trained) were sent to Korea in June of 1951. They were attached to the 3rd Reconnaissance Group on June 12th. The seven men and their dogs were: Cpl. William J. Irving, squad leader, from Tarrytown, New York who handled the dog Jon; PFC Huda L. Green, Kansas City, Missouri who worked Barrie; PFC Robert Bristol, Lincoln, Nebraska who handled Hamlet; Cpl. Virgil E. Price, of Wichita, Kansas with Leo; PFC Robert M. Potts, St. Louis, Missouri who worked York; PFC Larry B. Pollard of Detroit, Michigan with dog Orrin; PFC Farnia Rose, Davis, West Virginia and dog Pen. PFC Rose was also the veterinary technician for the dogs. (Stars and Stripes, 9/4/1951)

Pfc. Larry B. Pollard and Hamlet of 26th ISDP in Korea on November 3, 1951
US Army Photo by CPL Mervyn Lew (National Archives)

By July of 1951, they were already making the pages of local newspapers back home. PFC Green was shown with Barrie eagerly on the trail of Communist troops. Orrin and his handler, Larry Pollard, were given guard duty over the dogs' cans of horse meat. I suspect that the hungry Koreans would have found that dog food to be pretty tasty. The men were known to heat a can if the chow wasn't too good. Another picture in several newspapers featured Bristol and Hamlet, Pollard and Orrin, and Green with Barrie aiding a patrol on a scouting mission.

By July 12, 1951, two other men had joined the 26th according to a letter from H.L. Green (included in this chapter). PFC Robert A. Grossman was a combat trained dog handler and Quiller Coleman came on board as a vet tech. I'd sure like to know their stories but haven't been able to find any information on them or most of those first seven. We have a movie clip of Robert Grossman and the dog York from the National Archives which shows them riding a cable tram traveling up Hill 690. York was very good natured and willing to try about anything.

Crouching on left, Cpl Robert Grossman, instructor, watches as student SFC Dale Nix learns to heed warning alert of a scout dog on 14 February 1952.
US Army Photo by CPL Nathan Buchman (National Archives)

This first group was tasked with determining the effectiveness of scout dogs in the Korean terrain. Cpl. Irving was the right man for the job because he had been a scout dog handler during WWII. According to that Stars and Stripes article of 9/4/1951, Captain Frank J. Speigelburg of St. Paul, Minnesota was the commander of the recon company and was glad that these dogs were to join his patrols. He felt that the dogs would be especially helpful in the dark.

Sometimes replacements were not available from home so men were recruited out of line companies. Edward Fahey of Amsterdam, NY, Dale Nix of San Bernadino, CA, William Hoover of Ozono, TX, and Howard Butler of Effingham, KS, joined the ranks of the 26th in January 1952 in just such a fashion. The dogs went through a refresher course of basic training with their new handler to learn the sound of the new master's voice and build a bond with him. The dogs basically trained the new soldiers. Edward Fahey teamed up with Pen, Dale Nix worked with York, William Hoover worked with Hamlet and Howard Butler formed a team with Orrin. William Hoover transferred in from the 40th Infantry Division and stayed in Korea until the end of July 1952. He says Hamlet was already well trained when he got assigned to handle him. (Hoover, William letter Oct 2009)

The rest of the unit still at Fort Riley finished training and was shipped out in February of 1952. The next chapter will tell more about that first group. Madame Rosenburg and Colonel Ish continued to monitor the success of the scout dog program. The original study of the effectiveness of dogs in war zones established the cost savings and efficiency of operations. In response, Madame Rosenburg and Colonel Ish set up the Army Dog Training Center at Camp Carson, Colorado. Colonel Ish flew out to Colorado during the winter of 1952 on a C-47 military plane with about 20 German Shepherds. December 1st, 1952 was the beginning of scout dog training at Camp Carson.

Army Dog Training Center at Camp Carson
US Army photo by Mr. H.L. Stoddard

I am including a letter from Cpl. Green sent from Korea to the men coming with the first official platoon in February of 1952. It details supplies needed and specific areas of training to provide for the men and dogs.

Det. 26th Inf. Scout Dog Plat
APO 24 G-2 IPW
c/o PM San Francisco, California

12 July 1951

Dear Sir.

I don't know exactly what information you have received on the subject of activating your platoon in Korea, but we have official word of the change here. It came on a order from EUSAK and stated that the 26th Infantry Scout Dog Platoon would be activated in Korea. It didn't give the date or the organization to which you would be assigned. However G-2 of the 24th Division has requested you and feel sure that you will be put here as they are the ones who requested dogs when we were sent over and now have become accustomed to the methods employed in working dogs.

Since you will depart shortly I'm trying to pass on all the information I have that may be helpful to you.

1. Be sure that you bring enough tentage for all of your men. It is hard to get here and unless you have it with you, there is a chance that the men would have to sleep out until some could be found over here. We were here two months before we even got a Pup tent to live in.
2. Also if you come to this organization I have one good combat trained dog handler, Pfc Robert A Grossman, who at the present time is working York. Also we have a good Vet Thech, Quiller Coleman, who had five years experience in the work and is much better than Rose.
3. By the time you arrive we will have a definite answer on the questions of, what to do with a dog on patrol when the handler is wounded or killed. We have asked that it be left to the discretion of the man in charge of the platoon.
4. It is also necessary for your men to be very good map readers as they are the ones who have to lead the patrols. I am giving the men under myself this training now and they are becoming very good at it. Also in conjunction with map reading the men should be very adept at Infantry Tactics and procedures, conditions at all times.
5. Another thing recommended for your success with working dogs here is the ability to put over the dogs abilities and disabilities, to put there points over, a good plan is to continyue the policy we now have in

effect. That is to give demonstrations and practical work in classes to the men of the men of the units in reserve.

6. As far as promotions it will be easy for you or an officer to submit the names of your men to the 8th Army Headquaretrs. Our difficulty was having no officer.

7. We have found a process by which we get fresh hamburger for the dogs. When you arrive at your destination, contact Major Abbett, Ver. Feed Inspector, 548 QM depot, at Chunchon Korea. He will determine the amount you need and make arrangements for you to get it. He will also be your Veterinarian for serious conditions of the dogs.

8. We have got a request in through S-2 channels as to weather or not the Dog Handler are entitled to the CIB. Everyone here says yes but a definite answer has not come in yet. Will inform you if answer before or on your arrival.

9. All the dogs here are assigned to 8th Army headquarters work through 2 and 3 channels.

10. The dogs will only be used at night for patrols but in the event of a push be employed in the daylight for mopping up actions of enemy bunkers, this is the only day work.

11. The types of patrols on which the dogs are used here are (1) ambush. (2) Security. (3) Combat. (Cleaning up

12. They consist of:

(1) Ambush – Going out with a unit and carrying two dogs, handlers choose most favorable spot to work dogs and the dogs are worked in shifts of one hour each. The object of these missions are to kill enemy or take prisoners.

(2) Security – This type of patrol is to form security for our lines by contacting enemy patrols before they reach the lines. They are walking patrols and last about 4 hours.

(3) Combat – Here again is a walking patrol with only one dog used. The only difference is that a large body of men are used to contact and anihilate the enemy.

(4) Cleaning or mopping up work – Daylight work to check enemy bunkers after patrol for remaining Chinese.

13. We have good results on all these types of patrols.

14. The terrain here is a series of mountains and valleys similar to hill top pasture. The only patrols on the hills are the mopping up exercise, but these arn't many of them. The other are in the valleys at night. The valleys all have a small creek of river running through them.

They have many rice paddies, wheat fields, and corn fields in them as well as a number of deserted Korean homes. The wind here is generally from the north so it is almost always favorable for work.

15. Be sure and warn all men to learn to tell signs of booby traps and mines. As lead man in a patrol, they are our worse hazard. This is about all the information I have that hasn't been sent to you already.

H.L. GREEN
Cpl RA35750391
NCO

This was all helpful information. I just wonder why the tentage problem was not worked out since you will see that not having a tent was an issue again later. This kind of communication served to ease their transition into combat. The men with Cpl. Green were already due for rotation and so were not in Korea long after their replacements arrived. They were not there to accompany the new handlers on their introduction to combat.

The army considered these dogs as rather expensive and expected the handlers to take good care of them. Of course, the men grew to love their dogs and knew their life might depend on them. They actually were given general orders to follow.

A Dog Handler's General Orders

1. To take care of my dog and his entire kennel area.
2. To care for my dog in the proper manner, keeping him groomed always and observing him daily for signs of ill health.
3. To correct my dog immediately when he deserves it.
4. To praise my dog whenever he rates it.
5. To place the comfort and well-being of my dog above my own comfort.
6. To take my dog to a veterinarian, or authorized technician, whenever necessary, and see that their orders are fulfilled in detail.
7. To make no derogatory remarks about my dog at any time.
8. To agitate my dog unnecessarily under no circumstances.
9. To feed and water my dog properly every day.
10. To overwork my dog at no time, and see to it that he has proper rest and play.

11. To properly evaluate the powers of my dog, showing proper consideration for prevailing conditions, including weather, wind and terrain.

At the time we were in Korea, we were focused on survival and caring for our dogs. We did not always see the big picture. We wanted to help the Korean people and tried to assist the innocent victims. The little children were just pitiful. A lot of us gave them our C rations, and handed out clothes and food that people donated.

Picture of Korean children in 1953
Photo courtesy of Melvin Sexton

It was gratifying for me to have the opportunity to go back to Korea in 2003 as a guest of the Korean government with the Korea Revisit Program. I would recommend this trip to any of my fellow veterans. I was able to see the prosperity of the South Korean nation today and witness the freedoms and opportunities its citizens enjoy that they would never have under a communist government. The South Koreans are an industrious, polite, and tidy people. We returning veterans were honored by the respect and gratitude shown to us by all that we met, from government leaders to school children. I was able to witness the result of sacrifices made by our military personnel in the Korean War.

Chapter Four:

First Patrols

Prior to the arrival of the scout dog to the Korean War, probably about mid 1951, the war had reached a bit of a stalemate and consequently, more patrol action was used. The members of the 26th Infantry Scout Dog Platoon began their duty in Korea by educating officers and infantry men on how the scout dogs worked. Many people believed that the dogs would bark and just give away the patrol's location to the enemy. However, scout dogs were trained to be totally silent in combat and to alert to the sight, sound, and smell of unfamiliar people. During WWII on the Pacific Islands, some officers thought that the dogs should be turned loose to draw enemy fire so that they could locate the enemy. History shows that some dogs were killed by this action. Dog handlers had to demonstrate the unique skills of the scout dog and how to utilize them to save lives. The dog's sensitive sense of smell could be used to great advantage and they could hear three times better than the men. Last but not least, a dog seemed to have a 6th sense of danger. It took some time for the dog handler to familiarize himself with the attributes and characteristics of his individual dog. With time and experience, he was able to interpret the dog's actions and understand what situation likely triggered the alert.

I guess some mention should be made of one's first combat mission. You are usually very apprehensive. You would generally arrive at least three hours before the patrol was scheduled to begin and report to the commanding officer. He would introduce you to the patrol leader, maybe a sergeant or 2nd lieutenant. Some of the handlers had the misfortune of having a Major or Lt. Colonel as the patrol leader. They usually were leading a much larger group of men, and sometimes were less likely to accept the recommendations of a lowly war dog handler. These larger groups were often designed to make contact with the enemy instead of scout for information. It was really not that difficult to make contact with the enemy, and you certainly didn't need a scout dog to do so. Patrols with scout dogs were more effective at reconnaissance to gather information on enemy action and give early warning to the line.

After meeting your patrol leader, you then were introduced to the rest of the men on the patrol. The dog familiarized himself with all the members by sniffing them and identifying them as his team. Then you looked the country over with the map for the patrol and learned outstanding features of the terrain and landmarks. You had to get a picture in your mind so that you wouldn't get lost in the dark. If something happened to your patrol leader, you were second in command and responsible for bringing the patrol back to the line safely. For each patrol, a plan was laid out on transparent onion skin paper which was placed upon a topographical map of the area. This included numbered artillery concentrations, along with numbered land features, such as a burned out tank or a dead tree. You used these numbers to call in supporting fire by the artillery and then correct as necessary. The artillery usually sat back 3-4 miles and they could drop the fire in your hind pocket if needed. I am including a copy of one of my transparent onion skins which were laid over a map. By itself the onion skin would not tell the enemy anything unless you had the correct map under it. The patrol leader carried the onion skin to reference if he needed to call in artillery support.

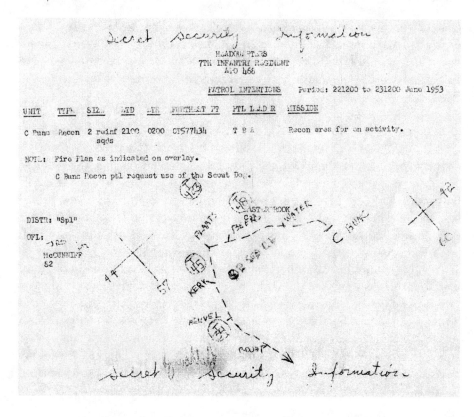

Onion Skin Map Overlay for one of Robert Fickbohm's Patrols

After familiarizing yourself with the men of the patrol, the terrain, and the purpose of the patrol, you usually had supper together and waited for darkness to fall. There was never what you could call a "good patrol", but they were good if you made it back safely. There was just more than a hundred ways to get hurt or killed in "No Man's Land". I don't know if I had any patrols without some scary incident. We dealt with mine fields, booby traps, the enemy trying to kill or capture us, and even friendly fire from our own troops. If it was possible, when a dog alerted or enemy contact was made, our patrol backed off because we were supposed to be doing reconnaissance. We were gaining information to allow our forces to be prepared for enemy action.

Clayton Haak says he had a total of about 30 night patrols which was about average for the first group. He says that as he was preparing for combat and thinking of how he might react and what lie ahead, he thought, as did probably many others, "I didn't want to be a hero but neither did I want to be a coward." This first group of dog handlers was unique in that they had no one to show them the ropes. Those first seven men had already rotated home, so our first full strength platoon went from safety to sudden combat. Their first patrols were nerve wracking learning experiences as they tried to figure out their role, the dog's working style, and at the same time, bring the entire group back safely.

The middle group each pulled about 35 to 40 patrols, as for my class about 12-15, and the last class for combat about 3 or 4. This does not include daytime patrols for infiltrators or terrorists who would sometimes set up a single machine gun on a service route, hence the need for a "shotgun guard" —not that they used shotguns.

Captain Richard Prillaman relates how having a scout dog along increased the confidence of the men in his command in an interview done in Fort Benning, Georgia after the war ended. "In late December of 1952, the 5th Regimental Combat Team occupied defensive positions southeast of Kumsong, Korea. The principal activity at that time consisted of numerous patrols, and frequent limited objective attacks. Chinese Communist Forces operated almost exclusively at night. During this period I was a platoon leader in Company L. Although they were highly efficient soldiers and were easily the superior of CCF soldiers in the daytime, my men lacked confidence in their ability to operate at night. The use of scout dogs greatly increased confidence in their own ability in night patrolling. Primarily, this was due to the fact that their fear of ambush was greatly decreased with the aid of the scout dog, and they were able to move more boldly and rapidly. After a few successes at night, they lost their awe of the enemy and were more efficient than ever, even when no dog accompanied the patrol.

The first time a dog was used by my platoon we were successful. Our mission was to move to the base of an enemy-outposted hill and set up an ambush for an enemy patrol. The scout dog platoon had just recently joined the division. Because this was to be a deep patrol into enemy territory, we were furnished a scout dog with his handler. The handler and dog reported to the company in the early afternoon of 27 December (approximately). I briefed the handler on the plan and the route, and then he suggested that I get the patrol together before dark so he could explain the manner in which the dog would be used on the patrol. The troops were allowed to pet the dog as he moved among them becoming familiar with the scent of each man that would be on the patrol. We moved out at dusk with the dog in the lead, because the wind was from our front, thus providing excellent conditions for a scent "alert". There was about a foot of snow on the ground. The moon was almost full, so that visibility was very good. With the dog in the lead we moved rapidly, setting up our ambush on a slope above a trail about two hours after dark.

The dog was located on the north side of our position where there were no friendly troops up wind from him. The enemy was expected to approach from that direction toward our front, therefore, I had directed the patrol's attention to that location. When the enemy appeared (a five man patrol), he was coming directly toward our position, moving on a cross country route at a right angle to the expected route of approach. The dog alerted first, and immediately the handler was able to point out the enemy to me before any other members of the patrol had seen them. Because of his early warning, I had plenty of time to alert my men and reorient their attention to the new direction. When the enemy was close enough, I gave the order to fire and the first volley cut down the entire patrol. We continued to fire until we were certain all five were dead, and then we began receiving quite a bit of fire from the outpost to our rear. We then returned to our lines at top speed with the dog in the lead.

I used dogs many other times after this incident and found them valuable in all cases. I have never known a patrol leader who was not pleased to have a dog along on his patrol." (Prilliman, Richard, Interview 1956)

My first patrol was at the side of a veteran war dog handler. I was able to observe and learn from someone who knew what he was doing – unlike our first group of handlers. I went out with Joe "Heavy" Thompson. Heavy was leading a patrol with his scout dog, Rusty. On this particular patrol, we were going to set up an ambush in a bombed out village. The village had a central square with only the foundations of the houses left. There was a dike built around the village to keep out the water from flood irrigation of crops. We were directly in that small square with no cover when the dog alerted. It looked like there was an enemy patrol behind the dike because the dog was pointing at it. We were in a precarious situation. We lay there and waited for them to fire over the dike so that we could pinpoint their location, but they did not fire. After about 10 minutes, we finally arrived at the conclusion that it was a very light patrol that did not want to engage a dozen of us. We packed our bags and went home (or at least back to the line).

Joe "Heavy" Thompson
Photo by Robert Fickbohm

On my first patrol with my own dog, Hasso, we got ambushed. I was leading a group of Belgium professional soldiers who were very competent. The wind was behind us and a light rain began to fall just as we got out in the valley. These conditions made it impossible for Hasso to work effectively. So I told the patrol leader "Don't depend on us, conditions are against us. Do as you see fit. We will be out ahead and doing the best we can." I don't know if he knew something I didn't, but I did not understand him well due to a language barrier. The patrol leader spoke broken English. For some reason he had his patrol in a skirmish line instead of the usual single file patrol line. But I was still out front a little bit. Two rifles and a machine gun opened up on me. I was just coming over a small rise and was only exposed from the belt buckle up. They shot just a little too high, almost put a dent in my helmet. And the patrol leader said "pull back, pull back, pull back". I hit the ground so fast that I left my helmet hanging in mid air. So I was busy looking for my helmet because they were throwing hand grenades and I thought I might need it. If they had been 10 yards closer, the grenades would have been coming over the hill. They didn't follow us; perhaps they were an outpost because they had 2 rifles and a heavy machine gun which night patrols didn't carry. We backed off about 200 yards and called in artillery support. And if they weren't dug in pretty tight, it went a little hard on them. That was enough excitement for the night and we went in. Much later I learned that many of the Belgium soldiers were convicts and if they completed their tour of duty, they would be free of further legal action.

Robert Fickbohm and Hasso
Robert Fickbohm's photo

Chapter Five:

Rest of Platoon Arrives

The remainder of that first group of the 26th Infantry Scout Dog Platoon left Fort Riley, Kansas in January of 1952. One of the soldiers in that group, Clayton Haak, tells the story well. "We finally left Junction City, Kansas with all of our equipment. And I mean all of our equipment: the dogs, their crates and equipment, men's equipment and luggage, and jeeps. We got on a train called the 'City of San Francisco' in Denver, Colorado. When we went over Donner Pass in the Sierras, there was snow as high as the train. We arrived at Camp Stoneman. From there we got on a ship called the Earlham-Victory. It wasn't a regular troop ship; we kind of hitched a ride over."

Ralph Trickey directs construction of a dog ramp.
Photo courtesy of Ron McKeown

"They gave us half a hold and in the other half was barbed wire, picket stakes, and 180,000 cases of beer. They had these commodities all sealed off. There was one guy who figured out that from the bottom of the hold, he could crawl up a chute (like a silo chute) and come down the other side of the hold. It was darker then the inside of a cow in there but he could take a case of beer, push it up the chute, and come down the other side with it above his head." The ship took the South Circle Route and the weather was great until they got about three-fourths of the way there. They encountered quite a storm, waves clear up to the pilot house. Clayton says that another of the guys, Hazen Stipe, "was too sick to die, he had to get better first."

Champ and Harry Ward on the ship Feb. 1952
Photo courtesy of Ron McKeown

Those who were healthy cared for and exercised the dogs but got a little
bored with the journey. Ken Strawder recounts one of the days that boredom
got the best of them. "Bruce Bushnell and I went to high school together and
we used to rodeo together. When we got in the army just 2 weeks apart, I
talked him into coming over to canines with me. When Trickey was at Fort
Riley, he said he could never tell what them damn two cowboys were going
to come up with next. Once Trickey sent us out to be a decoy for a tracking
dog that he was working with. We were out behind the horse barn where the
horses would come for water. The horses were retired but some officers would
saddle them up and play polo on the field. We also used that polo field to
train our dogs. So when he sent us out, and we saw those old horses grazing,
we took off our canvas belts, wrapped them around the horses' necks, and
jumped on bareback. We rode down quite a ways and jumped off. Then we
hid in the trees. The dog couldn't figure out where we went after the horse
field. Of course the dog wasn't trained to track horses. Trickey never seemed
to trust us after that. I wonder why?"

Ken Strawder and his dog, Ave
Picture from Ken Strawder

Ken goes on to explain what the cowboys did on the ship. "Well, on the ship, Bruce and I got a couple of ropes from the boats, quarter inch craftsman ropes, and made throw ropes out of them. We had to have something to do so the dollies on the deck that were used to anchor the boat to the dock were about 2 feet high and 6-7 inches in diameter and made a good target to rope. So other guys wanted to learn to rope. Well one morning we were just sitting on the deck after breakfast and the albatross were really close to the ship. According to the navy, albatross will stay with you. Bruce said, 'They are really close, I'm going to get one.' So he climbed up on the poop deck and swung at one. He hit the bird with the rope and it kind of dove down towards the water at a 45 degree angle. I swung the loop and I caught him around the body and one wing. He kept going down towards the water and the rope in my hand was getting hot as it went through. Another guy helped me pull him in and the cameras started coming out. The guys were saying, 'Them damn cowboys roped a gooney bird.' We stretched him out, Carl Claus had one wing and Clayton had the other. Somebody measured him and he had a 7 foot wing span and he was over knee high. A lieutenant came by and said, 'I wonder if he bites?' I said, 'Oh, no, he wouldn't bite sir', knowing dang good and well he would. Well that lieutenant stuck his finger in the bird's mouth. The bill was probably an inch and a half wide and 3 inches long. It came down on that finger and the blood flew. Anyway, the captain stepped out on the bridge and said, 'Turn that bird loose now' so we turned him loose. There was a navy myth that said as long as you've got the birds, they can't sink you with 10 submarines. If the birds leave, you might as well get your lifejackets because you are going to sink. Us poor old landlubbers didn't know about that myth but we soon learned!"

Claus, McKeown, Ward, Haak, & a deck hand
hold a gooney bird that Kenny Strawder roped
Photo courtesy of Kenny Strawder

Clayton Haak tells about the end of the trip. "Anyway, 18 days later we landed in Pusan, Korea. About the only way I can think of to describe Pusan is . . . if they had to give the world an enema, Pusan is where they would stick it! We got off the ship and they put us in a replacement company, and we had about 4 guys to a squad tent. I remember one morning, Kenny Strawder and I went over to eat at these picnic tables. They had hot eggs which I figured I would eat first so they wouldn't get cold, and before I could eat my cornflakes and powdered milk, they were frozen."

Pusan smelled terrible, all the sewage drained into the ocean. There was a similar problem on the west side due to a POW camp on the island of Kojedo that held 80,000 POWs. They contributed to the sewage problem, and the tide just washed all the pollution right back up on the beach. Pusan Harbor was like a big cesspool. The people of Pusan lived in little bitty huts with a hole in the middle with fire from a smudge pot. Our animals in the US live better than those people did."

The entire group of men and 26 dogs got on a baggage car of a narrow gauge train and headed north. It was very crowded and cold. They put the men's cots on top of the dogs' kennels. There was no heat and no windows. After a week that baggage car had a bad "air" about it. As they traveled, they saw evidence of heavy fighting all the way. The towns had been reduced to rubble, burned out Russian battle tanks were here and there. It was terrible but fascinating. For ten or twelve days, they only had C rations to eat. Sometime after arriving in Chunchon, Sergeant Trickey and the commanding officer went over to this replacement company and asked if we could get a hot meal. Clayton says, "I was never fond of Spam but that day they gave us a slice of bread with a big piece of hot Spam on it. I swear it was the best meal I've ever eaten."

left to right: Ralph Trickey, Hazen Stipe, Roy Thayer, Alton Rogen & Fox, Bruce
Bushnell & Hamlet, Clayton Haak & Wolf, Jack North & Arlo, Charles Armstrong
& Prince, Carl Claus & Rex at Fort Riley
Photo compliments of Clayton Haak

There was a delay while the 26th awaited orders. Sergeant Trickey
explains, "It was a supply problem. No one knew how the 26th was supposed
to be handled. We had to be attached to some company for food and supply.
We got to Korea and we didn't have one tent. It took us ten days and we
fought like heck but we finally had some tents to live in so they decided
we could move out." They went up to the Kumhwa Iron Triangle east of
Chorwan, just east of the last bend the Imjin River makes before it flows west.
The main service road was referred to as MSR. It was the main invasion route
when the war began. The 26th ISDP was split into 2 squads. The 1st squad
went to the 2nd Infantry Division and the 2nd squad was attached to the 40th
Infantry Division. The men and dogs began to give support to various patrols
as needed.

Left to right: Max Meyers and Stark, Ron McKeown and Champ, Clayton Haak and Tim, Bruce Bushnell and Happy, Fred Kraun and Toni, Charles Armstrong and Prince.
Photo from Ron McKeown

I guess the first incident I will refer to is an actual combat patrol. We were never allowed to write about patrols at the time of their happening because they were highly classified. This particular "after action report" was declassified after about 40 years and was discovered on the internet by my daughter, Sandra. I could hardly believe it, as Hasso was the dog I worked with on my patrols. A good dog, Hasso worked approximately 80 combat patrols without losing a man.

On March 26, 1952 in the vicinity of Kumwha, Korea, SFC James Heffron and his dog, Hasso, of the 26th Infantry Scout Dog Platoon were asked to lead a patrol. "The plan of the patrol was to set up an ambush for two to three CCF soldiers who had ambushed a friendly patrol the previous night. If possible the patrol was to capture prisoners. The formation of the patrol was to be single file, five yards between men, and myself and Hasso as point. At dark the group moved out on a finger which led down to a creek bed. Arriving at the creek bed the group proceeded up a trail which led north toward the objective. The wind was blowing gently from the northwest and this was excellent for Hasso. Hasso and I at point moved about five yards ahead of the patrol. At a point up the trail, Hasso gave me a strong scent alert. I immediately signaled the patrol to drop to the ground. I called for the patrol leader and told him that Hasso had given a very strong alert.

From past experience I knew that enemy were very close by and was pretty sure that they were located on a hill about 200 to 300 yards to our left. The patrol leader requested that I move in a little closer to the suspected area to pinpoint the positions. Hasso and I continued on to the base of the hill; the dog continued to alert me. Arriving at the base of the hill, Hasso lost the scent. I knew then that the enemy was up on the hill and not at its base. The scent had been traveling downwind from the hill because Hasso continued to raise his nose in the air to retain it. As we reached the base of the hill, the scent passed over his head. The patrol leader suggested that I go on up the hill to regain the scent. I objected to this because in doing so the dog would be practically on the enemy before regaining the scent from the angle at which the wind was blowing. The patrol leader asked me for suggestions and I told him that the best thing to do was to pull back out to the trail and see what the enemy had in mind.

The patrol pulled back to the trail and continued on its mission. Two CCF soldiers were observed on the hill as the group passed and this verified the dog's alerts. The enemy did not fire on our patrol. Moving on up the trail to a fork, Hasso gave an alert, this time he'd heard a sound. I knew this to be so as the dog did not scent but stopped instead and pointed in a direction toward the west. The wind meanwhile had veered and was not blowing from the east and I knew that there were no enemy on the right of the trail as the dog had not alerted. I again signaled for the patrol to drop to the ground and motioned for the patrol leader to come forward. I showed the patrol leader the direction of the alert, and he asked me if I thought we should continue on. I told him that I thought we might be walking into an ambush ourselves, as the enemy on the hill down the trail had had sufficient time to inform his forces of our presence. I suggested that in order to continue on that we move to the right and go around the alerted area. Agreeing on this, we started to move to the right. As we started up a trail to the right, fires from three machine guns and about five burp guns came into the area. The group hit the ground and took cover; no one was hit. The enemy fires were concentrated on the front of the patrol to prevent further movement forward. Keeping up this fire they then placed fire in the center of the group thus cutting the patrol into two groups. As this fire came in, the eleven men at the rear of the patrol pulled back and returned to Company L's positions on the MLR. This left six members and a dog without support. No communication was available as the radio operator had returned with the others. The patrol threw grenades at the direction of enemy fire and one grenade knocked out a machine gun. As the fire continued to come in, I commanded the dog, "Down and crawl!" The entire group then disengaged and crawled down to the creek bed, one at a time. This was done as the terrain was rocky and by standing up, we'd expose ourselves. Hasso and I were the last ones to get to the creek bed. Because the trail followed the creek bed, it was necessary to crawl about 150 yards before sufficient cover would be available and we could again stand up. Absolute silence was ordered in order that we could get out without the enemy finding out our plan. Moving along the creek bed, we reached a point which had sufficient cover and the entire patrol stood up. Hasso and I again assumed the point position. We continued on to the MLR position; there was no further contact enroute." (Heffron, James. Interview by Major Pierce Briscoe, Oct. 1952)

SFC Heffron and Hasso
Photo from Center for Military History at Fort McNair

Generally, the scout dog was most valuable in avoiding contact with the enemy. We preferred to obtain the needed information and return to the line without being shot at. The next incident I include is about one such patrol.

Another handler, Jack North, and his dog, Arlo, carried out a patrol on May 16, 1952 to reconnoiter a road and its bridges to determine if it might be used as a tank route north toward territory held by enemy. The soldiers moved single file with about seven yards between men. "The group moved out along the road and as bridges were encountered they were measured for width and their capacities estimated. This continued for about 2 hours and the patrol completed its mission and prepared to return over the same route to the MLR. I selected the point position as the wind would be blowing in the face of the patrol and this would be excellent for Arlo. The patrol began the return march. After walking about 26 yards, Arlo gave me a very strong alert. I signaled for the group to drop to the ground and motioned for Lieutenant Jordonnais to come forward. I told him that Arlo had given a very strong alert and that someone was immediately ahead but I did not know how far. Lieutenant Jordonnais deployed fourteen men on the left side of the road and two on the right. I remained on the road with Arlo. Lieutenant Jordonnais stated that the patrol was to remain in position until daylight. After about 30 minutes, Arlo, his ears pointed straight up, appeared to sense movement on the left. His head seemed to move as if he detected noises. No one in the patrol was able to hear a sound. About 15 minutes later, a noise rang out to the left front of the patrol followed by voices. The dog continued to point in the direction but no one could be seen. At this point the Lieutenant decided to move up the road to see if any enemy could be detected. Arlo and I accompanied him. We moved about 100 yards with no further alert from the dog. Returning to the patrol's position, Lieutenant Jourdonnais ordered everyone back on the road. The group returned to the MLR, without incident, arriving about 0100. It is believed that the alertness of the dog saved the reconnaissance patrol from certain ambush." (North, Jack. Interview by Major Briscoe, 10/30/1952)

Jack North
Photo from Ron McKeown

Arlo
Photo from Jud Taylor

Ronald McKeown, another of the first group of dog handlers, shares some remembrances of his dog, Champ. "In the summer time, I would take Champ and Jimmy (our Korean house boy) and we would head for a swimming hole in some river. It was strictly against regulations to treat the dogs like pets that way, but I felt sorry for Champ just chained up by his kennel day after day. There was one specific incident that triggered the need for those outings. After Champ and I had been on about 20 patrols, he seemed to become depressed. One day when I was field training him he started to sulk and even cut and ran back to his kennel. I guess dogs are like people. When they feel down and tired from all the pressure, they go back to where they feel safe and protected – home. We did a lot of romping and just plain old dog stuff on our days off after that episode. I was a pretty tough task master on Champ's training, which was continuous, so I felt it was good for him to just be 'DOG' for awhile.

One of the few fire fights that I was involved in occurred in an area they called the "Punch Bowl". It was extremely mountainous. When we saw the terrain first hand, we told the infantry commanding officers to which we were assigned that the dogs would be ineffective in this very steep terrain. They ignored our advice and ordered us out on patrol. We think they thought we were just trying to get out of dangerous patrol duty. I took one of the first patrols. Our lines were along a very high narrow ridge. The only way down into the valley was a slope of about 50 to 60 degrees. I told the patrol leader I would take the middle of the patrol. The patrol literally had to slide down the mountain on their backsides. Once we reached the valley floor, there was only a very narrow trail alongside a creek that had many large obstructive rocks, branches, turns and twists. It was about the darkest area I had ever been in. No sooner had we reached the valley floor trail and proceeded about 100 yards, when all hell broke loose with automatic gun fire and grenades going off ahead of us. I found out later that our point man ran smack into the point man from a Chinese patrol coming the other way down the same path. The GIs ahead of me in the patrol panicked and started running back down the path from whence they came, which meant they went right over the top of Champ and I. I had just dropped to one knee with Champ and was going to hold my position until I knew a little about what was going on. I was being knocked all over the place by our own guys. About the third time I got hit and decked, Champ's leash came off my wrist. I quickly surmised that this narrow little trail was no place to be, so I just started clamoring up the side of the mountain back towards our lines. Once I got about 100 yards up the hill, I stumbled onto a group of soldiers. Fortunately, they were on our side. We were all pretty stunned from all the noise and confusion. As I sat there I started to think of what I would say to my commanding officer, if I got back, about how I lost my US Army Scout Dog. In all of the melee, I had no idea where Champ was. Our little group was starting to get their wits about them again and we talked over what we should do. The patrol, as a unit, was completely broken up into very small dysfunctional groups.

As I sat there feeling very sorry for myself about losing Champ, I felt something wet and cold on the back of my neck. Yep, it was good old Champ. He just wanted to let me know that everything was going to be OK. I told our guys our best bet was to go straight back up the mountain and stay off of the trail. Our guys above us obviously knew there had been a fire fight and would be watching and listening for us to return. I told them I thought it best if we sounded off with our names every minute or so, so there would be no mistake about who we were. We got back to our lines, and Champ and I were both very happy to get back in that jeep and head for our home away from home.

Champ and Ron Mckeown, followed by Bushnell, Brazwell, Stipe, & Fahey
Picture compliments of Ron McKeown

Carl Claus and Rex
Photo compliments of Clayton Haak

Carl Claus was the trainer and handler of Rex, a very beautiful German Shepherd. Carl came from a small town in Iowa and was very well educated and well-liked. It was said of him that he read his Bible every day and when the going got tough, he always seemed to know the right answer. Carl and Rex trained together, worked very efficiently together, and lead their last patrol late on June 5, 1952.

Ken Strawder tells about that day. "We had a roster and when a call came in, whoever was next on the roster took the patrol. One particular afternoon two calls came in. I was first on the roster so I took the first call and Carl Claus got the next one. While the two of us were sitting in the tent at division forward, a knock came on the door (we had a wooden door like a screen door that you could knock on) and we hollered 'come in' and a captain and the general of the division came in. We jumped up and they said 'Relax, we just come up to visit'. They sat down on a cot and visited with us for half an hour. That was General Lemnitzer and I tell you he was one super good guy. Well that night we went on patrol. I went with the 55th airborne. They were on the line to replace someone who went into reserve. Carl was on the other side of the valley with the next company to the east. The valley ran north and south and was a quarter of a mile to half a mile wide. We were to set up an ambush position. Their outfit was going out on a patrol. They got into the Chinese but the Chinese got them first. They shot Carl and the dog, the radio man and the BAR man, all four. We could see the fire fight and hear the bullets over there but we didn't know what was happening 'till we got back in. We found out that they were shot up. The dog Rex died right away, Carl died shortly after. (So it was early morning, June 6, 1952) We went down the next day, Lt. Deaner and I, to graves registration, and there we identified the body. We had taken his clothes and belongings down with us. What this one doctor said was that he really died from shock. So anyway, that was the only combat loss we had in 500 patrols." Carl was awarded the Silver Star for Gallantry and the Purple Heart posthumously. Clayton Haak wrote a letter home in which he said that Carl was "the finest man I have ever known. I know one thing—he wasn't afraid of death. He wasn't depending on luck either, it was the 23rd Psalm: Yea, though I walk through the valley of the shadow of death, I will fear no evil for Thou art with me." No Man's Land could be called the valley of the shadow of death, for a lot of men, friend and foe, died there.

chapel for the ROKs
photo from Robert Fickbohm

A year after writing the account of Carl's death, I found a document from Maj. Gen. Lemnitzer that he had published for dissemination to all personnel concerned with the employment of scout dogs. It was dated June 16, 1952. He states that "Recent successes obtained from the utilization of scout dogs and handlers have effectively demonstrated the value of dog support on such operations. Several instances have been noted wherein maximum benefit was not obtained due to improper utilization of the dogs and a lack of understanding as to their capabilities and limitations." Later he states "Once the dog has alerted and the handler has interpreted the dog's actions to the patrol leader, then the mission for which they were attached to the patrol has been accomplished. They should at this time be moved to the rear of the patrol and obtain maximum cover." (Lemnitzer, Maj. Gen. June 1952) Brigadier General Wayne Smith wrote in response to the above directives that the patrol leader should "furnish the scout dog handler with one man for security. The handler cannot fire his weapon efficiently when handling a dog, therefore he cannot protect himself or the dog." (Smith, Brigadier General Wayne, June 21, 1952) Sometimes patrol leaders followed this advice, but in several instances, the handlers did a pretty fine job of hanging on to a dog and firing their weapon.

Unfortunately, accidents happen everywhere and Korea was no exception. One man, Howard Butler tragically died while waiting to rotate home, after pulling all his patrols safely. Mr. Strawder remembers that July 3, 1952. "We had a river that was about a hundred yards wide and on the north side it had a good beach. About two-thirds of the way across it got deeper and had a strong undertow. Three of us, Heffron, myself and someone else went swimming and lay around on the beach awhile. Then we swam back, dressed and headed back in. We passed Butler and two others going out for a swim. We had just got back to our outfit when we got a call about Butler. They couldn't find him. They had been swimming back but Butler was behind them. They heard the dog barking and looked back. They didn't see Butler. They swam back and the dog was swimming in circles. They could not find Butler so we all started looking. We had a half track on one bank and a tank on the other side. We tied a rope between them and put a guy every 3 to 5 feet. They hung on to the rope and tried to find something with their feet but had no luck. The next day, they found his body about 100 yards downstream where the water got shallower and there were some rocks. It was really sad."

Howard had earned the Korean Service Medal, The United Nations Service Medal, The National Defense Service Medal and The Republic of Korea War Service Medal. He drowned in the Hantan Chon River near Munggogae, North Korea. After his death, he was awarded the Bronze Star.

PFC Howard Butler and Orrin
US Army Photo, Atchison Daily Globe

Sid Nason went over to Korea the first time in early 1952 with Donald Smith, Lloyd "Pop" Coleman, Victor Brice, James Klenz, Robert "Chicken Rancher" Goodwin, Keith Smith, Jim Partain, Robert Haines, Reinhard Booth and Robert Willis. They flew on United Airlines from Travis AFB to Japan and then took a ship to Korea. The dogs all rode in crates.

The first group of men helped train these guys that came over, their replacements, but many of the new men had gun shy dogs so they had to give them their combat experienced dogs. Ken tells about one of the new recruits. "I took four guys, replacements, and my replacement had my dog. We did what we call a dismounted drill – sit, down, stay, crawl, jump, and all that good stuff. Bruce Bushnell had 4 guys and Jack North had four guys. And we stayed with our dog for two days and then we switched groups so we weren't with our own dog. The first day out my old dog Ave would go down but he liked to keep his head up, just a ways up off his paws. Sid Nason had him as Ave was going to be his dog. So I said 'Sid, make him go down'. So Sid took the choke chain down and the dog turned on him and jumped on his back. Ave grabbed him by the collar and had Sid on his back in a matter of seconds, sitting on him and growling. Sid's eyes were as big as buckets. And I didn't blame him much. I said, 'Ave, heel, sit' and he just stepped off of Sid and came back to my side. I said 'Now Sid, get up and string him up.' Sid said 'Hell, I can't even lift him.' The dog weighed 110 pounds! I don't know who ended up with him but that was pretty funny from my side. When we had the reunion at Fort Robinson, that was the first time in 50 years that I had seen Sid. I said 'Do you remember that?', and Sid said, 'You better believe it!'

I'll let Clayton Haak tell of his last patrol with Wolf. "My last patrol was off the north ridge of the punch bowl. The lines were quite close and very steep. You had to grab hold of trees to keep from falling. It was almost impossible to work a dog. We got only about three-fourths down the hill when we came under a lot of small arms fire. We got in a ditch about 3 feet deep. The bullets were hitting the bank behind us kicking up dirt. All of a sudden Wolf started barking. I guess he had had enough. I tried holding his mouth and ears shut but he was just wild. He was giving us away. The patrol leader and I discussed shooting him, but all of a sudden they quit shooting and he quit barking. We decided to try to get back to our line and luckily we did. The next day Lt. Deaner and I tested him. If I pulled my 45, he would try to bite my arm. So my patrols were over. Wolf was sent to Japan to be retrained as a sentry dog. I hated to see him go, and shed a few tears over it. He was my best friend.

Clayton's dog, Wolf   Clayton Haak
Both pictures from Clayton Haak

Our living conditions improved while we were there. At first we ate outside. It was hard to stay clean, etc. Each member went to Japan on R&R for 8 days after we had been on the line for 6 months. It was a ball, but hard to go back to Korea after that. Although living conditions were bad and at times things got pretty scary, I consider it the greatest experience of my life. We had a great bunch of guys and it was rare that there were any problems between us. We needed each other too badly. They were, and still are, the best friends I ever had."

Chapter Six:

Incidents, Firefights, and Just Plain Scares

Some of the boys seemed to just gravitate towards combat firefights and incidents, while others seemed to get through many patrols without stirring up much trouble. The 26th Infantry Scout Dog Platoon had a remarkable record for more than 1538 night patrols in Korea. Just think, that's like 1538 nights in no man's land. For myself, I only had 15 night patrols but that's still more than 2 weeks in danger. I never got scratched, but it seemed like something happened on almost every patrol.

We will try to share some of the incidents that resulted in silver stars, bronze stars for valor, and purple hearts. They are in no particular order so bear with us. If you served in the 26th, and your name doesn't come up in this book, rest assured we are not discriminating against you. It is difficult to accurately document everything that should be included in a book of this nature, and some of our men are rather quiet about their service. It's kind of like the dog, York. Everything he did seems to have been documented, whereas other dogs probably saved just as many lives, but you didn't hear about it. Just ask any dog handler, and they will tell you that their dog is the best!

Jack Wheeler was a well liked member of the 26th and still is today. It was said of him that when the going got rough, people looked to him for stability because of his integrity and honesty. I guess it was his faith and trust in a higher power, namely Jesus Christ and his heavenly Father. Anyway, Jack was on a recon patrol December 21, 1952 with 29 men of the 25th Division, 35th Regiment K Company. It was not a lengthy patrol as they left at 2120 and were back in by 2224 military time. After they were some distance from the MLR, Gray did alert. Jack and Gray were at point. Jack asked the patrol leader to come forward, and Jack told him the estimated place of alert. Then Jack and Gray moved back about 3 paces. The patrol leader chose to move forward and the patrol only went about 30 to 40 yards when all hell broke loose. There was a lot of small arms fire, mortar and flares. The Chinese flares were sort of yellow and our 81mm flares were very bright. I remember when moving on a patrol, if you heard them "pop", you had to beat them to the ground or you were really exposed.

Back to the story, at this time Jack and Gray made a dive for a ditch which they discovered was already occupied by a Chinese soldier. When he saw Gray, he panicked and ran. He disappeared. A little later, this lieutenant came over to Jack and asked him to load a clip in his rifle. Jack said he was not about to, as he had a dog in one hand and a carbine in the other. He didn't intend to let go of either. He was trying to protect Gray by holding him down, as he wanted to look around and see what was going on. After holding out for some time, a tank finally rumbled out there and the Chinese fled. At the debriefing, it was determined that Jack and Gray's alert, and Jack functioning as a rifle man saved a lot of that patrol. They wrote him up for the Bronze Star with the V device. Jack and Gray were another of our great teams.

PFC Jack Wheeler presented with Bronze Star for Valor by Maj.Gen. Samuel T.
Williams (to Jack's right is Johnson and to his left is Partain)
US Army Photo by PFC William W. Jones, (National Archives)

Robert Goodwin was awarded the Silver Star for his actions on December
19, 1952 near Chorwan. Even though he was under enemy fire, he used a
bayonet to probe his way through a minefield that had already blasted the
patrol leader and one other soldier. He was able to rescue the two wounded
men. They were Puerto Ricans from the 65th regiment. Robert also acted as
the unit's veterinary technician since they had no veterinarian.

Robert Goodwin presented with Silver Star by Maj. Gen. Williams
US Army Photo by PFC William W. Jones, (National Archives)

On October 24, 1952, Cpl Larry Piatt and his scout dog Charlie went on a routine recon patrol with the 7th Infantry division. Sidney Nason was to be shotgun guard for Larry and Charlie. It was his first patrol. The conditions were not favorable for the dog. The wind was from the side towards the front so Larry and Charlie were situated third from the front in a patrol of 19 men. They were on their way out and very close to the main line of resistance, perhaps only 100 yards or so away from it. No one was really ready for action yet. But Charlie looked down a brushy slope and gave an alert either from a scent or a sound he heard. Larry saw the dog's alert and said, "Hold it!" and they all hit the ground. That's when the grenades began coming in. Larry and Charlie became separated in the explosion and Larry was trying to get reunited with his dog. He remembers seeing someone spin and fire a burst with an M2 carbine. It had to be Sidney Nason because he was the only one with an M2. The rest of the patrol had M1 Garands or M4 Grease guns and carried 45 pistols. Larry made a leap to get to Charlie and the second round of grenades came in. One landed on the opposite side of Charlie and he took the brunt of it in his chest. Larry said the Chinese charged them twice. Nason continued firing even though he was wounded and his M2 had come apart so that he was holding it together with his hand. His hand was badly burned and is still curled today to fit an M2. Larry's M4 was lost in the grenade explosion and he was firing with his 45 pistol. Larry dragged Charlie back a ways, and Nason dragged a couple of guys back towards safety. After getting back a little, someone got on the field telephone and got the tank on the line above them to direct fire on the Chinese. This broke the fight up and the enemy left. It was estimated that there was about 75 enemy soldiers in on the attack and a screening patrol the next morning found 30 of them dead. Our patrol had 13 out of the 23 men wounded in action and Charlie was killed in action. Even though Larry was wounded in three places, he still carried Charlie back to the MLR. "The whole patrol gave Charlie the credit," he said. "If it hadn't been for him, we would have walked into the ambush and gotten slaughtered." He still wishes he could have done more for Charlie. He has fond memories of his dog, a Bronze star for Valor, and a Purple Heart.

Larry Piatt and Charlie
Cropped from group photo from Jack Wheeler

Sid Nason has the Silver Star for gallantry and a Purple Heart for his wounds. Both men came back to the unit after time in the hospital. They helped to train replacements; one of which was me. Larry also worked training the dog Jigger who went on to be a good scout dog. This has been my most difficult account to write because I had three accounts by war correspondents and two personal accounts to try to compile. I hope to honor the memory of Charlie who gave his all. I hope this does justice to both men as I consider them both to be very dear friends, brothers, and buddies.

Sgt. Sidney Nason is congratulated by Maj. Gen. Samuel T. Williams, 25th US Inf. Division after being awarded the Silver Star
US Army Photo by PFC William Jones (National Archives)

Major General Samuel T. Williams was admired by the men of the 26th ISDP. Some considered him the best general they ever had because he took care of his dog platoon. He didn't let anybody mess with them. When he wanted something done, they were going to do it for him. They also thought highly of General Maxwell Taylor. He felt that the dog platoon was an asset to his soldiers.

Victor Brice was in a firefight about October of 1952. It was said of him that he was perhaps a little too brave and one would hate to slight a man for that. His buddies say he didn't hit the ground fast enough when the action occurred; he was busy pulling the trigger. As usual, Brice and Flash were at the head of the patrol. Flash had alerted the patrol, but a lucky shot hit Brice before he hit the dirt. He died beside his companion, Flash, who was not hurt. Flash was a very good scout dog but a little savage. When the men of the patrol tried to help Vic, Flash was trying to defend him. They had to throw a sleeping bag over him and wrap him up to transport him back to the 26th. He was very protective and didn't think he should leave his master. A couple of the guys should have gotten Purple Hearts for dog bites! Brice was a good soldier who deserved the Purple Heart given to him posthumously.

Back: James Klenz (WIA) , Victor Brice (KIA), Robert Willis, James Kunberger
Front: Robert Haines, Jack Wheeler, Grey, Robert DeLille
Picture compliments of Jack Wheeler

Champ was a German Shepherd war dog and as much of a professional soldier as any man in the 26th Infantry Scout Dog Platoon. One dark night, with the temperatures dipping to near zero, Champ and his handler, PFC James Klenz, led a patrol (Champ's 39th patrol) out into enemy held territory. They had only gone a short way when the ground exploded beneath them. They had stepped on a mine. Klenz tried to piece together what had happened. He only knew searing pain and the fact that his dog was bleeding to death. He begged someone to put Champ out of his misery and then passed out. He awoke in an Army hospital and for him the war was over. The mine he stepped on had shattered both of his legs, and made it necessary to amputate one of them. He mourned the loss of his team mate and friend. Cpl. Reinhard Booth expressed it like this, "It's hard for an outsider to understand how we feel in these circumstances. The comradeship welded together between man and dog is an inseparable one that surpasses human ties of friendship." (Stars and Stripes. 1/18/1953)

Reinhard Booth, Sidney Nason, Jack Wheeler bury a hero, Champ
US Army Photo taken by PFC Charles Multz (National Archives)

These three soldiers had the solemn task of burying Champ on a frozen hillside. They observed a moment of silence for war dog Champ and marked the grave with a handmade marker. It stands as a reminder of the supreme sacrifice made by a soldier in the service of his country. Klenz was from Wisconsin and was deceased before we were able to locate him and become better acquainted.

James Klenz
Photo from Clayton Haak

Champ smelling daisies
Photo from Ron McKeown

Chuck Hunt shared an experience on one of his patrols. "One night I was with a group from the 25th Division. I forget what company it was. The area we were at was in the Kumwha Valley. The reason they wanted a scout dog and handler was that they had lost 2 patrols. They never come back, just disappeared. So they wanted to find out what was going on. And it was in the same area where the enemy held Sugarloaf Hill. I think what happened was that they must have come off of there and intercepted our patrols. I believe what happened to the patrol I was with answered their question. We were going out, and we were probably half way from where we really wanted to set up when we heard someone follow us. My dog, Major, let me know there was somebody coming, so we stopped and waited for awhile. But the dog wasn't too excited, so we finally went a little farther but only about 50 yards. Then he got really excited so we stopped and lay down. Pretty soon we heard them and when we got a crosswind, we could smell them. There was snow on the ground and it was spotty, which was a good thing because Major was black and white. There were light spots where the snow was, and dark spots where it had melted. It was probably the last of February or the first of March. We just stayed completely still. I took off my coat and laid it over my dog because I thought they might be able to pick him out.

Shortly after that these Chinese came in and set up around us. This was about ten at night. They didn't even know we were there but they just started setting up in a circle, like an ambush. In fact, the way I was facing was good because if I had been laying the other way, a guy would have stumbled over my feet. We lay there without moving until the enemy moved out—about 4 o'clock in the morning. It was a long night but I didn't get cold, I was too nervous. The main reason we were there was to find out what was happening to these patrols. What I believe was happening was that a patrol would go out, and while they were gone, the Chinese would come in and set up an ambush. They would capture our patrol on their way back in when they weren't expecting anyone and were starting to relax. I think that was the deal. The Chinese were very good at ambush, very quiet fighters.

The fact is when I was up in the 25th Division, we went on a patrol and some of our people left their grenades and stuff out there. I told them the Chinese will sneak in, collect them, and just throw them back to you the next night. Sometime we were just careless about laying things down in the dark, and forgetting them. That reminds me. We used to have a jacket that we all wore on patrols, an overcoat for when it was cold. I wore it one cold night. I put my hand in the pocket and was feeling around when I felt a pin from a grenade –just the pin. I have never been so scared. I was afraid to move, thinking a grenade was going to go off, but I didn't know which one to grab and throw! I decided to feel all the grenades to see if one was missing a pin. There were 3 grenades in that pocket and they all had a pin. Come to find out, the guy that wore it the night before had used a grenade and had stuck the pin back in his pocket. I was sweating that night let me tell you."

Charles Hunt   Major
His photo   photo from Charles Hunt

I never would carry a grenade because I was afraid that fire from a burp gun would knock the handle off and I'd get killed by my own grenade. The bullet proof jacket would stop the bullets from a burp gun, but wouldn't help you if your own grenade exploded. Besides, I couldn't throw very far. One night, two guys from my group, Shafter Eversole and Larry Gittelson, were coming back down that road that was posted: "You are under enemy observation. Go like hell." The Chinese had pretty much zeroed in on that road. They were driving as fast as they could and a pin came out of one of their grenades. Eversole said, "What am I going to do with this?" Gittelson yelled, "I don't know but get rid of it." Eversole threw it out the window and they managed to get out of range before it exploded.

Conrad Hamp or "Hamp" as he was always called came from Kentucky. He was a regular army man and had done one hitch in World War II and was on his second hitch in Korea. He was there during the hard winter of 1950-1951 when China intervened. He was one of the finer pistol shots that I ever saw in the army. I would say that he was the best in our outfit, because I think maybe I qualified as close second or I wouldn't know anything about it. He got his Purple Heart on a patrol with the 25th Division around the end of February or March. He got a few burp gun bullets in the leg, but they didn't hit any bones. Hamp was a good scout dog handler and a soldier that spent a lot of time serving the good old United States. Every time he got drunk though, Jud Taylor would have to ride herd on him to keep anyone from getting killed. One night I was writing a letter when I realized someone was coming back home because I had Hasso right beside me. Hamp tried sneaking in the back door. Hasso went for him which he should have if someone was sneaking up on me. Hamp pulled his 45 and put a slug right between that dog's front paws. Lucky for him, he didn't hurt my dog. All of our dogs were protective of their masters and anything that belonged to that master. Basically, Hasso felt he had to guard anything I tied him to. I would loop his leash over the shifting lever of the jeep and no one would steal my transportation. I was going out one day and an MP asked me where my shotgun guard was. I just pointed at my dog and said "That's my shotgun guard." He let me go on by.

Top: Alvin Steeneck, Clyde Treece, Robert Willis, Conrad Hamp
Bottom: LeRoy Ross, Ted Mitchell, David Hull
Photo compliments of Clyde Treece

We have another incident here that is probably not on paper anywhere. I spent some time in 2000 with Jim Partain. He was one of the handlers of the famous dog York. There are several stories about York, but sometimes the ones done by the media were not accurate. This one I heard from the horse's mouth so I'll include it in this book.

York and Partain were out on a patrol one night. And they were out there quite a long way. The patrol leader kept looking at York. And he said, "Are you sure he don't see something?" Partain said, "No, he don't." Then a little later on, the dog was kind of halfway alerting. The patrol leader suspected that the dog heard something. He asked again, "Are you sure he don't see nothing?" Partain said, "Yeah, he is alerting but I think it is one of our own patrols. I don't think it is enemy." The patrol leader was irate about it. "There is no one out here but us and the enemy. We need to open fire on them." Partain said, "I don't think we should do that." The guy was insistent about it. Finally Partain said, "Why don't you send three guys up there to that ridge to do some observing to determine who it is and what they are doing? Yes, there is someone out there, we know that." So they did that. Well, it was a patrol from the next company down the valley and they had gotten off course. This time if it hadn't been for York we would have fired on our own patrol. York saved us from our own people instead of the enemy. It's just as important to identify our own patrols. This is a credit to York because you can never fool these war dogs. When you had one alert, you knew what it was. They reacted differently to friendly patrols than to enemy, especially the Chinese. In this case, York did.

On another occasion, York saved a patrol of 15 soldiers from being ambushed. The group left the MLR just after dark, weary from the bone chilling wind and headed toward the Chinese lines. York was nervous from the start. Some 200 yards beyond the Allied lines, they came to a bridge over an icy stream. Just short of the bridge, York pointed his nose towards the stream bed and tugged hard at his harness. "I said to the lieutenant, there's something there and it's not far away", Partain related. York was right. One group of Reds was waiting in the stream bed at the right of the bridge and another group was hidden in an orchard to the left. They were waiting for the patrol to get on the bridge to blast it in a deadly crossfire. Instead, the patrol hit the dirt and the lieutenant called for flares. A minute later a flare lit up that dim little section of the Chorwan valley as bright as daylight. "We shot them up and then moved back," said Partain. "With our reinforcements, we were able to get them to withdraw and we continued on to our original destination. If not for York's warning, we wouldn't have called for flares and we would have walked onto the bridge." (Stars and Stripes, 2/23/53)

James Partain and York
Photo compliments of Jim Partain

This is a story that kicked around our platoon for years. But forty years later, I couldn't come up with the name of the man or dog until one of our reunions. Before Ted Mitchell died, he sent his memoirs to Jud Taylor and Jud brought them to me. The story goes like this:

"One of the tactics we used was baiting the enemy. A patrol of 50-100 men would go out into no man's land and, at a predetermined location, set up a defensive position. Then the dog handler would go out with two other soldiers and sweep an area of 200-600 yards distant. If the enemy was detected, the patrol would notify the main body of troops and they could either ambush the enemy or call fire on them. Once or twice this procedure went wrong. I remember one incident when the Chinese, by infrared detection or other means, had surrounded us. We were clear out by the Chinese lines that night, so close that we could hear the Chinese talking in their trenches. All of a sudden the dog started alerting. He went around in a circle as he alerted. Sure enough, we found out that, even as dark as it was, and without a shot fired and nothing said and all was quiet, the Chinese had us surrounded, right up next to the Chinese lines. And so we thought about it awhile. The dog continued to point out each Chinese soldier to the handler. As we watched Vetter pinpoint the location of each, we found out that there was a slight gap between two of the soldiers with a small draw in the middle. Ted and Vetter pointed down this draw. By following the dog and crawling down the draw, we got away from the Chinese. Before the Chinese knew what happened, we were out of range."

The Chinese had just been waiting for daylight to come to capture the US soldiers. They would have had to surrender because there were so few of them and they were so far from their own lines. In this incident, Vetter got them out of a very bad situation.

Ted Mitchell and Vetter
Photo from his daughter, Roxanne Key

Leroy Ross was a fine soldier. He was awarded the Bronze Star just before he went home and he deserved it more than I did. He pulled all his patrols and was friendly to everyone. On one of his patrols he got slapped by some shrapnel in his hand. It swelled so bad he couldn't use his hand or hold his dog. They took him to first aid and Sgt. Cheatwood had to go get that dog.

LeRoy Ross just after receiving his bronze star.
Photo compliments of Roxanne Key

Happy was another dog that did his job well. It seems that Happy started as a sentry dog, but he did not excel at that. Maybe his disposition was too gentle. But as a scout dog, he was like a duck to water. He was trained by Ron

McKeown and then his next handler was Donald Stahl. It is estimated that he pulled 87 patrols, and he brought them all back.

It was said by Alvin Steeneck, his last handler, that Happy saved a light patrol from ambush one night by alerting so they could pull back. Later that night, large numbers of enemy soldiers were sighted in that area. On his last patrol, on May 3, 1953, they were returning from a routine ambush patrol with Happy and Steeneck on point, when Happy suddenly froze on the spot. This was a different kind of alert for Happy but Steeneck knew there was definitely danger ahead. Alvin coaxed the dog to "search" further but he would not budge. Alvin advised the patrol leader to back up and reroute. The patrol leader did not heed the warning and proceeded. He took only three steps before he triggered a booby trapped grenade. Our dogs were not trained to detect booby traps so Happy had probably not alerted by sight or smell, but by some sixth sense that dogs have about danger. A number of dog handlers would attest to that sixth sense. Unfortunately, Happy was killed and the patrol leader and Alvin Steeneck were quite badly wounded. So Alvin had a Bronze Star for Valor, a Purple Heart, and the fond memory of a very special scout dog.

Alvin Steeneck

Happy who was KIA
Photo from Jud Taylor

Chapter Seven:

Ambushes and Minefields

On the evening of April 16, 1953, Cpl. Jud Taylor and his scout dog, Baron, led a recon patrol from Company C out past the main line of resistance near Unjan-Ni, Korea. The patrol was suddenly attacked by three reinforced platoons of enemy forces. In the initial phase of this attack, five men of the patrol were killed in action, and eleven were wounded in action including Jud who took some shrapnel in the shoulder. One man was reported as missing in action. Jud and Baron promptly moved into a forward position in order to provide security and warn of further attacks. The dog was wounded immediately and unable to be of assistance. Baron was separated from his master by a grenade explosion which temporarily knocked out Jud. Having lost his dog and painfully wounded, Jud nonetheless remained with the patrol until dawn, fighting to halt the enemy advance. After daylight, a commanding officer noticed Jud was wounded and ordered him back to the line for medical attention. Baron was found in no man's land 2 ½ days later and was rescued by Baker Company of the 15th regiment. He was treated for wounds and blood loss by Sgt. Robert Goodwin, veterinarian for the 26th. Jud was happy to welcome Baron back. The small patrol was responsible for killing approximately twenty-one enemy and wounding another thirty. Jud Taylor received a purple heart and a bronze star for Valor.

John S.D. Eisenhower awards Purple Heart to Jud Taylor
photo from Robert Fickbohm

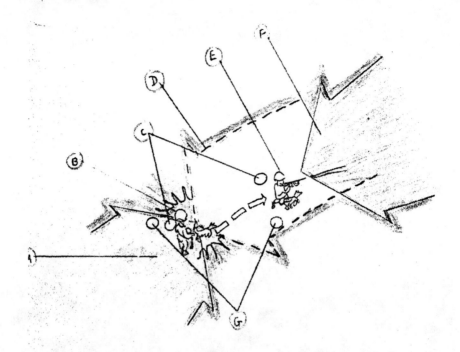

A. Friendly patrol attack by three hostile platoons
B. Cpl Taylor and his dog during first attack
C. Positions of Lt Juston during action
D. First hostile attack inflicting many casualties on patrol
E. Cpl Taylor, although wounded, moved to a forward position to warn patrol of further attacks. Even though dog was wounded on second attack Cpl Taylor remained and fought side by side with riflemen.
F. Second hostile attack in which Cpl Taylor lost the use of his dog.
G. Positions of Pvt Beaudion during action

Drawing Showing Action on Jud's Patrol
From citation, compliments of Susan Taylor

Charles Hartnell was leading a patrol back to their lines when the patrol leader couldn't find the safe lane through a mine field. Daylight was coming and they had to get out before it got light or they would be decimated. Hartnell pointed his dog, Jack, towards their own line and told him, "Let's go." He let the dog lead him through the mine field, step by step. After they were safely through, they looked back and saw that the entire patrol was frozen in place. They had been too afraid to follow them. So Hartnell and the dog had to backtrack through the mines to rejoin the rest of the men and convince them to follow. I guess they decided if the dog made it through twice, then hopefully he'd be successful a third time, so they followed step by step. That dog led them all back safely.

On a later patrol, Hartnell led a reconnaissance group out through a bombed out village. They stopped to rest and Hartnell sat on a piece of foundation. Suddenly mortar rounds began to come in. His dog gave him a huge jerk and he fell off his seat onto his entrenching tool and he hurt his back. The dog had alerted on a battalion sized group of enemy. They were in the middle of an enemy push and promptly headed back to the lines to warn them. There was almost no time to prepare, so Hartnell and the dog became part of the front line defense and he took a machine gun tracer completely through his thigh. It missed the bone and seared the flesh so it didn't bleed. He saw no reason to go to the medics so he did not get a purple heart at the time. He later applied for and received the Purple Heart, maybe 3 years before he died.

Charles Hartnell
Photo from Robert Fickbohm

There were many instances when our scout dogs made it possible to avoid an ambush set up by the enemy. A number of times, a patrol was able to reverse an ambush after the dog located the enemy by simply setting up your own ambush and waiting for them to come out. There were so many more options available when your dog let you know exactly where the enemy was located.

In the last 3 months of the war, we had six men wounded in action. Some authors who have written about the Korean War said this time period was kind of a stalemate but for us it wasn't. We really got shot up.

Dale K. Robinson was a man from a little town in the northwest corner of Houston, Texas. It was sprawled over by Houston and I never have been able to locate Robinson. When our bunch was training with the dogs, Dale was in the 1st squad and a few of us would go up there and he was trying to teach us the card game, Casino. He didn't get finished before he got sent over to the 25th Division TDY and the rest of us were with the 2nd Division.

Charles Hunt was the NCO in charge of that little group of about 5 men. Dale and his dog Arlo were leading a patrol about the 15th of June 1953. Charles and I believe that Dale's patrol must have been spotted by a good forward observer of the North Korean or Chinese artillery, and the patrol took a heavy barrage of large mortar or artillery. He never came back to our unit because he got a pretty large piece of shrapnel in his forehead. He wrote a letter to somebody in the unit that he was in a forward MASH and they were going to put a steel plate in his forehead. That was the last we heard of him. I really took a liking to that boy and he and Arlo were another very good team.

Front: Philip Little, James Wommack, Joe Thompson
Back: Unidentified and Dale Robinson (WIA) with our 6x6
Picture from Sid Nason

On June 10th of 1953, Philip Little was on a recon patrol on the east edge of the Chorwan Valley with the 25th division. There were 11 men on the patrol. Philip's dog was Ave and he alerted. The lieutenant in charge of the patrol did not believe that the dog was correct and continued on. The Chinese had set up an ambush and they opened fire. During the fire fight, this lieutenant came up missing. The assistant squad leader got on the telephone to call for assistance, and this lieutenant actually answered the phone back at the position of the support group. They never found out if he had bugged out on his men during the fight or if he simply went back for the support. However, he did not attempt to call for help on the phone like his assistant did. Either way, this small patrol was pinned down without their leader. They didn't know where to go, or what to do so they simply held their position and tried to protect themselves. During this fight, Philip caught a piece of shrapnel just below the right eye which cut the optic nerve and left him blind in that eye. He says that the first thing he thought of was an old sheepherder he knew who was blind in one eye. He figured if that old guy had gone through life that way, so could he. A support group got out there and held off the Chinese so that the remnant of the small patrol could get back to the line. Two of the men were killed in the action and eight were wounded. Ave was a very good dog and he and Phillip had done their job correctly. They should have been able to pull back and avoid the confrontation. Philip was evacuated for medical care at a MASH hospital, and spent some time in a hospital in California before being released from the service. He currently has a ranch east of Sheridan, WY and a beautiful white Great Pyrenees sheepdog.

With the training we were given and the jobs we were assigned to carry out, we should have had more rank to go with it. We should have been able to participate in the decisions made which affected the lives of the patrols we were trying to protect. We needed the clout to deal with situations like Philip Little encountered where the officers ignored the advice of the dog and handler. When I began leading patrols, I had heard several accounts of patrols that got into trouble because they did not heed the dog's warning. I made the decision that if I was working the dog on patrol, I would not follow the order to move into danger. If I had to march that officer back on the point of a bayonet, I would not let him send my men to their death. I would rather face a court martial if it would save my life, my dog's life and the lives of the men I was there to protect.

Top: Shipman, Maupin, Hermanson, Walker, Clifton
Bottom: Taylor, Hartnell, Cheatwood, Thompson
1953 Korea picture compliments of Susan Taylor

One of those wounded was John Clifton. He was in my dog training class which was conducted in Korea by our 26th veterans after they completed their combat tour of duty. This was a very effective method of instruction. We listened carefully because we knew that they had survived. We didn't just learn about our dogs, but also do's and don'ts while on patrol. Our class trained about late May to the middle of June. Action was pretty heavy at this time with Purple Hearts coming down like fall leaves. We were an attentive group of men! John Clifton was to be our veterinary technician but he had to go through scout dog training and lead 3 patrols before he assumed his position. Unfortunately, his 3rd patrol got caught in an ambush. They were trying to capture the dog and patrol on this very dark night so they used grenades, both fragment and concussion. Clifton and his dog, Stark, took quite a bit of grenade shrapnel in both of their behinds. Stark went to the Air Force Veterinarian and John went to MASH. Both were back to assume their duties in about three weeks. John had been interviewed because he had worked for a vet. He became our vet tech for the dogs.

Back Row: K.Hermanson & York, M.McFarlane & Ajax, R.Fickbohm & Hasso,
L.O'Connell & Rusty, Instructor J.Cheatwood & Jack,
Front Row: J.Clifton &Stark, W.Morning & Roggie, R.Kornder & Major,
CO Lt. L.Suiter & King
Robert's Photo of his class, Arrived in Korea May 1953

1st Lieutenant Leo Suiter went through scout dog training with our class and chose to lead 3 combat patrols before he took command of the platoon. He was a POW in WWII in the Battle of the Bulge and returned to fight again in Korea. In 1944, he was with the 106th Infantry Division and they were in reserve but running patrols to the front lines. Leo tells about the situation like this: "We woke up one morning about Dec. 17th and there was shooting going on all around us. I told my platoon sergeant "it sounds like we are surrounded" but he answered, "Well now, we are all right." We were the contact between 2 regiments and could hear the battle going on down in the valley. We heard our guns last, so we figured they got what they were shooting at so we started to come down but lost contact with our unit. We kept moving around trying to regain contact and as we followed a fence going over the hill to a wooded area, the Germans were shooting at us but they were not very good shots. We stayed in that wooded area over night. The next day we went around back to where our headquarters used to be but they weren't there. As we maneuvered around, we found places where people had been captured and had just dropped their weapons and stuff. Well we came to another wooded area and the Germans were in there and started shooting at us. They hit one person on the far side and he went down. They sent the medics to pick him up. Our second Lieutenant said. "Well they know we are here so we better keep moving." We were still trying to make contact. We came to this little l-shaped group of trees. I was the 3rd man back, kind of single file, and the Germans hollered "halt" three times. We hit the ground and they threw a hand grenade. It killed the first man, and hit the 2nd and the 4th man in line, our platoon sergeant who was behind me. Well, my feet were towards the woods so I turned into a crab and I headed back towards those trees. They shot up a flare so, of course, we just gave up. But the men in the back started hiding in the haystacks. It so happened that this was a horse-drawn artillery and if it had been daylight we would have whipped them. But in the dark and confusion, we didn't know what we had gotten into. It was the element of surprise that got us captured. The next morning the Germans went down to pitch hay for their horses and started digging the other guys out of the haystack. I don't know of any in our group that got away.

They carried us down to an area where we started grouping up. We had members of the 104th Airborne, 3rd Armored and our unit: two regiments of the 106th, about 10,000 of us marching back towards Germany. Every time we came to where we were supposed to catch a train, the Americans had bombed there so we kept marching. I believe it was Christmas Eve, when we came to an area where we could stop for the night. My unit went in a large building of concrete with a round roof that had the windows boarded up. We hadn't had anything to eat except some sugar beet scraps that we picked up along the road. Well, they had 2 types of sugar beets and one of them made me sick so I quit eating any of them. Anyhow, the next morning the dive bombers were coming in and bombing. They didn't know we were there. An incendiary bomb hit the round top of our building, knocked a hole in the roof and came on in. It didn't hit anyone but the pressure was so great that the windows blew out and the GI's started going out the windows. Those Germans weren't about to stop us either and they started marching us out. We marched all day but got nothing to eat. We were guarded by the regular German army and they were just regular soldiers. They didn't treat us too badly. Now if we came onto some SS troops that was a different story. We had nothing to eat, but they had nothing to give us. We crossed the bridge Koblantz and went into Germany. We finally got up where we caught a train and they loaded us in a cold, cattle car. When we went through Berlin, the bombers were bombing but we didn't get hit. But they kept us moving on. We went to Stalag 4B and were processed. They had a good many British and a good many Americans in that camp. The people in that prison camp looked like they were getting fed well. I don't recall getting a meal from the time we were captured until we got to Stalag. We did get some good meals there but we didn't stay there long. I guess there must have been about 150 of us that got sent to work camps. And there our diet was a bowl of soup that looked like the dishwater they had washed their dishes in. It didn't have much substance and we got a half slice of black bread the Germans made. That was our diet for the day and we would go out and work on projects they had. Then it wasn't long until the dive bombers were coming in. We knew the Americans were pretty close because the P47s only flew about 60 miles from the line. That was 2 weeks before we were liberated. I was taken off the work detail because my legs were swelling. I would lie around until I knew the French doctor was due to come along and then I would get up and walk around until my legs swelled back up again. This French doctor said it wasn't the result of malnutrition, it was dry beriberi. About a week after we got word that Roosevelt died (so it was about April 19th, 1945), the 89th division came across the hill and we saw them coming. As soon as they started coming down the hill, the Germans got us out and marched us out to the edge of town and they disappeared. When the commander was trying to get his troops into town, we were blocking the way. So he said "Get out of the way, we have to secure this town. Go back to where you were because my men have orders to shoot anything that moves in this town." So we went back to the building, but then we snuck all over town trying to find something to eat. Soon they moved us into something like an apartment building. We started getting trucks to move back. We had several truckloads of us and we got back to a staging area where they would fly us out in C37s. Well we got back to Paris and got set up and had to ride streetcars whenever we went out to get a meal. We got some Red Cross donuts. A couple of people almost foundered. Then we caught a ship back to the states.

I applied to OCS and got in. I later got ordered to go to Korea and was assigned to a security platoon of the 2nd division. Word came around that they wanted somebody to take over leadership of the 26th Infantry Scout Dog Platoon and my name came up as someone who had been raised on a farm. Cheatwood came up and interviewed me. He asked me if I drank beer, and played pinochle and when he found out I also played guitar, he gave me the job and I took over from Lt. Kunberger in 1953. They were a well trained group of men and they loved their dogs and read them well. I am confident that those dogs saved many lives.

I thoroughly enjoyed my time with the 26th. Of course, it helped that we had a little spring to keep our beer cool and the veterinarians sometimes brought steak for the dogs. That's where I learned to cook steak. "

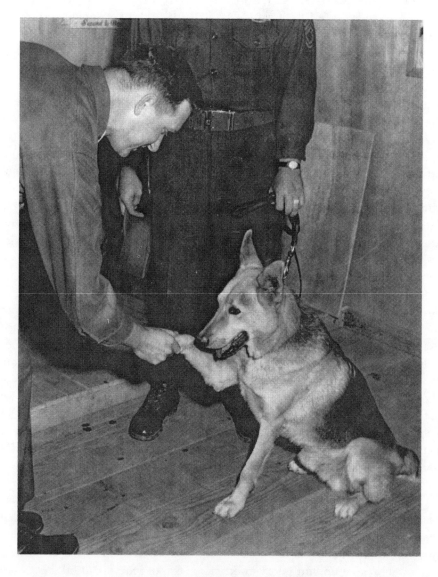

1st Lt. Leo Suiter shakes hands with Tim
Photo from Leo Suiter

I was out one night in the Kumhwa Valley and Hasso alerted. "There's Chinese up over there," I said to the patrol leader. Let's pull back." We did and called in the artillery on this position. This was such flat land country and this was going to be close support, so we lay in the lowest place we could find, the creek, right up to our ears. They put those artillery rounds just exactly where we wanted them, they were right on target. Things were pretty quiet for a little bit. I had a new green lieutenant that night and he said, "Let's go over and see what that done." One of the guys from Ft. Riley had told me about a similar situation where the artillery had not wiped out the Chinese and when they advanced, they had been ambushed, so I said, "Oh no, we have all night. Let's just back off and observe for awhile." Well in about half an hour, low and behold, someone in fire control got mixed up and we got five more artillery rounds in the exact same spot. If we had moved up, we would have been right in the middle of it.

Another incident took place July 25, 1953, two days before the treaty was signed. Our unit was in the west center on the MLR, in what was referred to as the Iron Triangle. This was the furthermost north position on the MLR about 12 miles north of the 38th parallel. The 25th, 3rd and the 2nd Infantry Divisions had been in position there. Our unit, the 26th Scout Dog Platoon stayed in the area and worked with whatever division was in place there at the time. The 3rd Division was just moving out into reserve when the Chinese attacked the South Korean forces to our right. They were overrun and pushed 10-15 miles south, and it would have been further except that the 3rd Division was ordered to get behind them and stop this advance, which they did. After the smoke sort of cleared, the 3rd wanted a couple of men and dogs to do night patrol work up front to see what the Chinese were up to, and I and my dog were one of them. What a mess things were after that retreat and we had to go through it at night. We had to go through the 3rd Division, the Korean units, and of course, some of the Chinese were in this area too. All were equally dangerous in the dark with no established lines. Well, we didn't detect any Chinese activity on our prescribed route so we lay on the side of a hill and rested before we started back in. We sent 3 men to the top of the hill to do some observing. Apparently the Chinese were on the other side of the hill and heard us. The Chinese were known for their accuracy with small mortar rounds, and they started firing them over the hill. Our patrol was scattered along this hill about 100 yards and one of these mortar rounds hit a man at the far end. I looked over at my big German Shepherd and he was digging frantically. I knew that he knew the next round was ours. I just grabbed him and hugged the ground tight, sure enough the next round landed about 8 feet from us but on the uphill side. We got the dirt but the shrapnel whizzed over us. If we had been still sitting up, we would have never survived unscathed.

There were about 5 rounds in all, but no one else was wounded so we got the heck out of there. If it hadn't been for my great scout dog, Hasso, I wouldn't be around to tell this story.

Robert Fickbohm and Hasso
Photo from R. Fickbohm

Chapter Eight:

Communication and Recreation

When not on patrols, the men of the 26th trained their dogs and took care of them. But time still weighed heavily as they yearned to be back home with loved ones. Communication was an important part of their lives. For something to do, and to get news of what was happening in the states, soldiers swapped addresses of sisters and cousins and wrote to each other's friends. Well I opted to write letters rather than spend too much time in the NCO club. Actually, even though I was engaged at the time and wrote to my fiancé, Elaine, every night and probably mailed it every 2 or 3 days, at one time I was writing to six different girls besides the one I was going to marry. Elaine and I kept all the letters we received, and it became almost like a diary of the events in our lives. She sent me the following poem while I was overseas, we don't know who wrote it or where she copied it from but it certainly expresses the feelings of the women left behind.

"Loving a Soldier

Loving a soldier is not always gay,
For with the price you must pay—
It's mostly loving but not hold;
It's being young and feeling old;
It's sending a letter with an upside down stamp
To a far-away lover in a far-away camp.
Being in love with merely your dreams
Brings thoughts of heaven with love light gleams.

It's having him whisper his love for you
And whispering back that you love him too.
Then comes a kiss, a promise of love
Knowing you're watched by the God above.
Reluctantly, painfully letting him go
While you're crying inside – wanting him so.

And days go by. No mail for a spell.
And you wait for word that he is well.
And when letters come you shiver with joy
And act like a child with a new toy.

It's loving a soldier, the boy you adore;
And hating the world, yourself and the war.
And it's going to church, to kneel down and pray
And really mean the things you say.
And though you know he's far away
You love him more and more each day.

Loving a soldier is bitterness and tears
It's loneliness, sadness and well-founded fears.
No! Loving a soldier is no fun;
But it's worth the price when the battle is won."

Author unknown

Robert Fickbohm and his fiancé, Elaine Hanson
Picture from Robert

Ron McKeown's wife, Jeannie, kept all of his letters too and these letters became a historical first person account of the events of the war during the time he was there. Of course, we were not allowed to tell much of what we were doing since we were usually working with intelligence, and our letters were censored. One of Ron's letters tells about a form of recreation many of our men enjoyed: hunting. "Max and I were walking up the draw to act as decoys when a pheasant flew in front of us. It lit on the side of a hill about 100 yards from us. I didn't have my carbine with me but Max did. He took a shot at it and missed. It didn't bother the pheasant at all. He just kept walking along as though nothing had happened. Max took another shot, and we both thought he had missed again. The pheasant flew straight into the air and dropped. We ran over to where it lit, and there it was hiding behind a rock. We went in and grabbed it. We looked all over it for a wound, but couldn't find any except a spot on its head where the feathers were missing. The bullet had just grazed his head and only dazed him for a few seconds. When we got back to the tent, we went down to the mess hall for cooking utensils. Kraun got it skinned so we threw it on the skillet. It was a good effort but the meat was tough as hell. Later we had a hunting party with better results."

"I had signed up for a recreational hunting trip. We formed a line with about a 10 yard space between us and started slowly walking up a grassy hillside. We got about half way up and a small deer jumped up and started running. The unfortunate part was that the poor thing took a course that fully exposed it to all our guns right on down the line. We all took a shot at the deer that you see on the front bumper. It is an adult deer. We were told that Korean deer are much smaller than what we see stateside. Even without a war going on there is very little for the deer to eat."

Hunting party: Ron is second from the left, the rest are not from the 26th
Photo from Ron McKeown

Sometimes there was organized entertainment for the troops brought in by USO. They were always appreciated and had a very good show for us. One of the highlights was Marilyn Monroe. You probably can't see her in the following picture. My daughter-in-law, Anne, wanted to know. "Why didn't you get closer, that picture could be worth some money?" Heck, 2000 GI's were all trying to get a lot closer! There were other shows as well. Since we were next to 3rd Division band, they had a band shell and outdoor seating on some logs. The place was called the Bulldozer Bowl.

Marilyn Monroe is center stage
Photo by Robert Fickbohm

In the summer time, we went swimming either at the swimming hole or the Imjim River. One day Larry Gittleson was making a real nice swan dive at the hole and he didn't come back up. We were almost ready to go in after him, when he came up all bloody. He had gone too deep and hit a rock and split his head pretty bad. Guess he didn't check the water depth first, it was only about seven or eight feet deep. The dogs enjoyed cooling off in the swimming hole, too.

Our private pool
Photo by Robert Fickbohm

All of the men speak highly of the Korean people but especially those who served them as "house boys". These young men would attach themselves to a group of "GI's" and perform chores to earn some money. They did laundry, shined shoes, and cleaned up around camp. They also fed the dogs which was a pretty big job. The money the soldiers gave them did much to improve their living conditions and was a tremendous help to the families. Jimmy was one special houseboy to the soldiers there in 1952, 1953 and 1954.

Jimmy is still around in January 1954 to play the part of a "line crosser" for visiting media! Ollie Hermanson with York, and BJ Maupin capture him.
US Army Photo by M/SGT Cordeiro (National Archives)

Ron McKeown can tell you a little more about him. "Jimmy was with our squad all the time we were in Korea. He was a joy to all of us, a wonderful young boy with a great smile and personality. He was also a very good worker. We would all argue over which of us was going to adopt him and take him home with us. He loved to go to the swimming hole with Champ and I. Once I took him to Seoul to visit his family which he had not seen in months. Our squad paid Jimmy well and he was a good saver, so I am sure he wanted to give his family money to help them through the worst of times for them. Seoul, back then, was a swarming, dirty, bombed out mess of a city. Jimmy directed me through crowded narrow streets with many turns. I was busy trying to memorize right, then left, then another right when all of a sudden Jimmy jumps out of the jeep and hollers back to me as he disappeared into this mass of humanity . . . 'pick me up right here tomorrow at noon'. The next day I was really worried if I would make all right turns to find the same corner where I dropped Jimmy off. I found a spot that looked familiar and parked. I was a few minutes late in getting there, and as the minutes ticked by I began to wonder if this was the same corner. I was about to start a circular search pattern for Jimmy. I began to think how I was ever going to explain to the squad that I had lost our house boy in Seoul. Then as quickly as he had disappeared the day before, he reappeared out of the din with the famous Jimmy smile on his face. He thanked me all the way back to our squad tent. He told me that his family was very happy to see him, and was so grateful for the money he left them because they were out of money to buy food with."

Ron and Jimmy hit the road to visit Jimmy's family in the summer of 1952.
Photo courtesy of Ron McKeown

Lee carrying laundry.
Photo from Orv Anderson

Lee's name was something like Li Ki Jon so the GI's called him Leaky
John. He was a great worker. There was an older man that we called Papa
San whose name was Che. He was sort of in command and was responsible
for the younger house boys and he made himself accountable for anything
that might be solen or work not done. It seemed watches, billfolds and other
valuables were never missing whereas in some other units, like the 3rd Division
Band Color Guard, the houseboys only stuck around long enough to find out

where everything was and then they would be gone with everything they could get their hands on. Of course, they were never seen again. Papa San was in charge of hiring and knew where to find honest men. We had great houseboys with whom we formed lasting friendships. Some men tried to look them up when they returned to Korea on a Korea Revisit tour almost 50 years later but weren't able to find them.

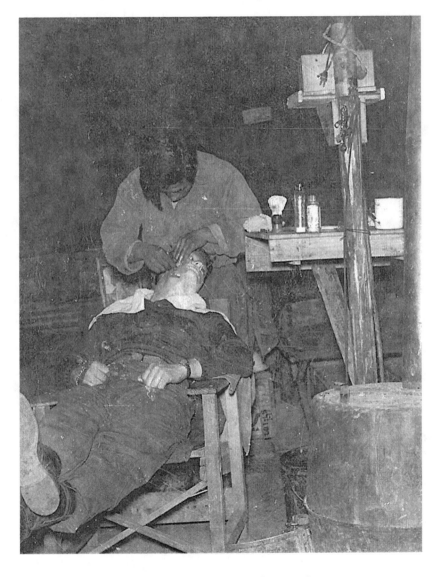

Che gives Orville Anderson a shave in the tent.
Photo courtesy of Orville Anderson

One of the most popular visitors to the 26th Infantry Scout Dog Platoon was John S.D. Eisenhower. He was quite impressed with the scout dogs and handlers, and as G2 in charge of intelligence for the 3rd Division, he occasionally called upon them for a mission. He seemed to be happy and comfortable with the regular soldiers and would visit them and play guitar with them. What made him even more popular was that he would bring a quarter of beef, and we'd have a barbeque. It was even better when he brought girls too. Some of them were musically inclined. Third Division band was there and performed. It was not a big, drunken party either, just eating, music, fun and gaping at the girls.

Eisenhower in the back ground. Others unidentified.
Photo courtesy of Jud Taylor

Even when there was no one but our platoon, we enjoyed music. Eversole, Cheatwood, and Lt. Suiter all played guitar. Jim Partain played one as well when he was there. I played a little harmonica, but hadn't yet realized that my harmonica only played one key, C, and so I couldn't accompany a lot of songs. So we had lots of caterwauling. I remember Robert Goodwin, AKA Chicken Rancher, picking and singing into the wee hours of the morning. At that time, he was getting close to the end of his patrol duty and some men got kind of nervous towards the end of their duty.

Suiter and Cheatwood tuning up.
Photo from Jud Taylor

Occasionally, all this music was not very appreciated. We were sometimes out almost all night on a patrol and liked to sleep in a bit the next morning. 3rd Division Band was right below our tents and probably never stopped to think about us sleeping when they came out to practice in the morning. Well I had been out all one night, and was abruptly awakened by this guy blowing his toot flute right up towards me. So I got up and went out, grabbed a rock, and threw it at him. It almost went right down his horn. I knew what was going to happen – a delegation would be coming up the hill – so I headed over the hill in the opposite direction and right on over to where we trained the dogs. Sure enough, the delegation proceeded to the C.O. tent and Lt. Suiter tried to find out what happened. Of course, nobody knew anything and I didn't "fess up" either!

3rd Division Band
Photo from Jud Taylor

Ken Strawder tells about requisitioning needed supplies. "Max Meyers wasn't a thief but things just seemed to stick to his hands. We had 5 gallon water cans that we used to water the dogs and for storage. Max said that it would be a good idea if we could get a trailer like what they have for the company areas; they held more like 300 gal. They were on a trailer that you pull behind a truck or jeep. We asked if he was going to go through supply and he said, 'Naw, I'll just keep out a watch for a water trailer.' There was a water site with a water purification system where the trucks would pull up and leave their water trailer for filling. The area also had barrels for fuel and diesel so the drivers would go up and refuel their jeeps or trucks while they waited for the water trailer to be filled. Max was just sitting in the jeep in the trees and when one guy dropped off his trailer, Max drove down and hitched it to the jeep. He drove back into the trees where he had a can of white paint, a brush and a stencil. He quickly painted on a fictitious number and the letters ISDP. So here he comes with a water trailer with a little bit of fresh paint. That poor guy is probably still trying to find his water trailer. It's hard to call it a combat loss when you're 10 miles behind the front lines. (You can put that in the book. It's true and a lot of people did stuff like that during the war.)"

Sometimes this was called requisitioning supplies. Charles Hartnell was great at that. Before he left, he told me I should go over to officer's mess as they got a little long on some things. He was a friend of the mess Sgt. so I went over there. While we visited, his men were loading stuff in my truck. When I got back to our place, I discovered that I had 750 pounds of coffee in 30 pound Navy tins. At one point we had 6 jeeps, one of which was a Marine Jeep.

It was a good thing we had those jeeps, sometimes they became the casualties of war. Sid Nason says "One night, Eversole took the wrong road and ended up front of the lines just before dark. The Chinese were embedded all over that mountain. The Chinese opened up fire on that jeep. They shot it all to pieces but them guys got out and jumped in an irrigation ditch. They crawled along that ditch until they could get close to an infantry trench and dove in with them. They radioed back to us to get a jeep up there and get their jeep out. They got the black light out on me and Goodwin as we went out there to try to get a look at that jeep and see how we was going to pull it on out of there. Along came a South Korean Dodge single axle truck loaded with rice, just moaning and groaning along there, and it run over the good jeep. I tell you there was rice everywhere. Pop Coleman was the head of the motor pool and read them the riot act for messing up our jeeps." ("Pop" Coleman was a WWII veteran and he was the staff sergeant.)

BJ Maupin and Roger Kornder
Don't remember which buddy gave me the picture.

Once again the cowboys in the group devised their own brand of entertainment. How about this early version of the mechanical bull? Our boys could always find a bit of entertainment to be had at the NCO Club: good, bad or otherwise. Wrangler BJ Maupin was down there one night and 187th Airborne was there in force. They were positioned on the MLR straight north of us. Anyway, he made a comment that would have been better left unsaid, and he really took a beating. His face was swollen so bad in the morning, he couldn't dress right for formation. Sid Nason says that one night, "old Cheatwood got drunk and he fell down. He rolled all the way down that hill. They finally picked him up and brought him home in the jeep. That was some doing."

Sid also "felt sorry for old Stark, I let him sleep in the sleeping bag with me. I'd talk to him and he got real comfortable with me. He knew me real well, but if I tried to get him off my sleeping bag, he would growl at me. It was like 'Don't mess with me now, I done got comfortable.' He got to where he couldn't go on patrols. When you put that harness on him, he would get to wheezing so bad, it was too loud to take him on patrols."

On New Year's Eve in 1953, the captured Chinese dog, Jack, kept drinking beer. He must have had about seven cans. He started chasing cans around the tent, tipping over bunks and stuff. Finally, we had to take him outside and tie him to his doghouse. We went out to check on him a little later, and the top half of him had fallen out of the kennel and his head was resting on his crossed paws. He was snoring like a drunken sailor.

Christmas in combat was, and still is, difficult for a soldier. We all wished we were home with family. I recently found a letter amongst my mother's things that I had written home to my folks on 26 Dec. '53. In it I wrote, "I guess I may as well do a little writing. Everybody but three or four of us are getting drunk. And they have been drunk since Christmas Eve. And of course, this Christmas Eve was about like the last one for me. Only this time it was a little more dangerous. Naturally, lucky me had to get a patrol. It was about as far north as the Chinks would let me. We were to have a party that night but they sent six of us out. (Those six dogs and handlers went out with different patrols.) They were expecting an attack that night. They had seen fifteen Chinks the night before so everyone was armed to the teeth. Three of us were out there by ourselves, we walked a long ways but we didn't see anything. We were looking for them, hoping we wouldn't see anything.

Christmas wasn't too much over here although we did get a good dinner. I will send you the menu, it wasn't quite all that was on the menu – that just makes it sound good when I send it home. The big package you sent came the other day. Everything was in good shape and thanks a lot."

Eighth United States Army
Christmas Dinner
Korea   1953

Shrimp Cocktail - Crackers

Roast Tom Turkey

Sage Dressing - Giblet Gravy - Cranberry Sauce

Snowflake Potatoes - Buttered Peas

Hearts of Celery - Carrot Sticks

Olives - Pickles - Cole Slaw

Parker House Rolls - Oleomargarine

Hot Mincemeat Pie - Fruit Cake

Assorted Fresh Fruits - Assorted Candies

Mixed Nuts

Coffee - Milk

Our Menu for Christmas Dinner in 1953
Copy from Robert Fickbohm

Some of the guys and I did get to go to church the 27th. We tried to attend as often as we could. Church in Korea reminded me of the pilgrim days. Everyone took a rifle or pistol with them. It was army regulations, and not a bad idea. The enemy liked to attack when they thought we were celebrating or relaxing. After the war was over, we helped build a Quonset Chapel for Division Headquarters. They would have several services per day to accommodate different denominations. It may be that in a war zone, men become a little more devout in their faith. One of our fine young men, Robert Bollschweiller, felt very fortunate to have his dog, Tim. "He related to us how he prayed before every patrol, particularly for his dog, that he might be keen and alert, and that all concerned might be inspired to do those things which would serve to accomplish their mission and preserve their lives." (Mortensen, Benjamin June 1997)

And let's end this section with what was one of my personal favorite ways to pass the time.

Robert Fickbohm in the hammock
(No, I am not responsible for all the empty beer cases.)

Chapter Nine:

Truce and Deactivation

The last day of the Korean War is a date I won't ever forget. The truce was signed in the morning of the 27th of July, 1953. It was supposed to go into effect at 22:00 hours that night. I don't know what caused it, but the Chinese and the US Artillery started throwing everything they had at each other. It sounded like they were trying to blow them guns up! We had a 105mm battalion behind us about a fourth of a mile. Every time they fired those guns, our tent would go "woosh". When they fired all six guns at once, the noise was awful. Down the road I could see enemy artillery shells bursting, and by the middle of the afternoon, there was so much smoke from the incoming and outgoing shells that it was just hazy. That whole valley was filled with powder smoke and noise; you can't imagine the noise. At the time, I thought the Chinese were just firing randomly but that was not the case. I had been up there two nights prior to this one, and I knew the ROK's and the 3rd Infantry were sitting on top of the ground, just foxholes and no bunkers. But I didn't know the Chinese artillery and mortar had them zeroed in. There were a bunch of men killed, and many, many wounded. I didn't know how bad it was until last winter when I met Chaplain Mortensen of Utah who had been up there with the 3rd ID. It didn't look like there would ever be a truce, the fighting intensified. At 22:00, all of a sudden it became deathly quiet, just deathly quiet. No one said anything, we just looked at one another.

The next morning, the Chinese soldiers and the American soldiers were out in "no man's land" swapping cigarettes and that sort of thing for souvenirs. Can you believe that? That actually happened; they were out there to see each other. Later the big brass said we shouldn't do that because we couldn't trust each other, but spontaneously, that's what they did.

Robert Fickbohm kept a copy of the newspaper account of the truce signing.

I guess this is probably the place to tell about the last combat event, although it happened after the truce was signed and the war was over. Well, the powder smoke had hardly cleared before you could smell shoe polish and we had to start training again. First we all had to be briefed on the Armistice Situation and new rules of combat. I had to sign that "I have been oriented thoroughly and understand the provisions of the Post armistice situation as it applies to me and my conduct." Quite a few of our combat veterans had time enough in country to qualify for early deployment home. So we were training replacements and patrolling the demilitarized zone. We were worried that the enemy would use the truce as an opportunity to regroup, so we didn't take much time to relax.

Anyway Roger Kornder and his dog, Major, were out one night and so was Shafter Eversole and his dog, Stoney. Now Roger was on a patrol with the Thailanders that were attached to the 2nd ID. At this time, there was a heavy penalty for carrying a loaded rifle or firing one, we had only unloaded rifles and a fixed bayonet. I rather think some of our allies were not complying with this order. Shafter was with a United States patrol. Somehow the two patrols ran into each other in the dark. Neither dog alerted because they knew each other, and knew there was no danger. In the dark and confusion, one of the US boys in Eversole's patrol shot Roger. He didn't realize they had run into a UN patrol and was probably young and nervous. Roger recognized them as a friendly patrol and hollered out and stopped any further shooting. If he had been unable to stop them, there would have probably been more wounded or killed. I think the Thailanders were loaded because I was out in their area one night and they warned me beforehand that if I heard anything that sounded like "Halt", I better stop and have my hands up. I did hear "Halt" and got my hands up, but I was looking into a machine gun. If it wasn't loaded, why was the guy sitting behind it?

Roger was shot in the upper arm with an M1 Garrand but it missed the bone. They had to walk quite a way back to the line and then he went out by ambulance to a Mash hospital. He doesn't remember how Major got back to the line. (Sgt. Cheatwood frequently went and got the dogs whose masters went to the hospital. Sometimes he got pretty chewed up.) The young man who shot him probably had to answer for why his gun was loaded and why he shot one of our own soldiers. Roger was back to the platoon in about a week, but a nerve was cut and his right index finger has very little control to this day.

Roger and Major just after Roger came back.
Photo from Robert Fickbohm

Working with an aviation company, the 26th Infantry Scout Dog Platoon devised a way to quickly transport a scout dog and handler to an area that has need of their services. Larry Gittelson says they designed a cage of chicken wire and light wood which could be quickly mounted on the litter pods of the army's H-13 helicopter. Cpl. Keith Hermanson of Lignite, North Dakota and his dog, York, showed how the process worked. When a call came in for a scout dog team to locate an unidentified person that had been seen in the 2nd Division area, they demonstrated the effectiveness of such a delivery method by boarding the helicopter and quickly rounding up an "unidentified person" before sundown in a dress rehearsal for the 8th Army. (Stars and Stripes, 2/12/1954) As far as we know, our platoon was the first to deliver a handler and scout dog by helicopter. This allowed quick response to a request for a K-9 team. This is where deployment by helicopter got its start and it became common practice for our boys in Vietnam.

M/Sgt. James Cheatwood, Cpl Larry Gittelson, 2nd Lt. William Walker of the 26th ISDP with Major Jerome Feldt of the 2nd Aviation Co.
US Army Photo by PFC Bob Sholes (National Archives)

After the cease fire had been signed, the 26th carried out security patrols for the Quartermaster around the camp, because the Korean people were so poor that they would try to steal things they needed. One night, Jay Bowers and his dog, Major were out on patrol. Major stopped and warned Jay not to go on. Jay tried to move around him but the dog would not let him. Jay then discovered that there was a precipice that dropped some 30 feet to water below. If he had continued on, he would have fallen over the edge. Major saved him from serious injury, if not death.

Jay Bowers and Ajax, Don Secrist and Orrin
Photo from John Drives

There were different reasons men volunteered to work with dogs. Dale Thompson tells how he ended up with the 26th ISDP in Korea.

"I got my Draft notice in February and had to report on March 12, 1953 in Plankington, SD. From there I went to Sioux Falls and then flew to Ft. Sheridan, IL. I spent two weeks there, learning to march and getting uniforms and stuff like that. Then I rode for two days on the train to Ft. Riley, Kansas where I spent 16 weeks in basic training. After Ft. Riley, I got about two weeks of leave. During my leave, just two days before I was to report back, the truce was signed. From home, I went back to Sioux Falls, flew to Minneapolis and then to Seattle/Tacoma airport and reported to Fort Lewis, WA for a couple weeks. From Ft. Lewis, I went by bus to the docks in Seattle. There were several buses of us, but my bus was in a wreck which made us very late getting to the ship. We were the last to board before the ship left. We spent fifteen days on the ship and arrived in Pusan, Korea. Then they put us on a train for about 36 hours to Headquarters Co. 2nd Div.

Everyone, who had gotten on the ship earlier than my busload, had orders, and were sent to the infantry. The twenty that were on my bus (that had the accident) were in a group which Lt. Leo Suiter came to interview.

He asked if there was anyone who did not like dogs. A few of the guys said they didn't. His next question was 'Is anyone against drinking?' A few more raised their hands and he told them to go. Then he asked 'Does anyone like to play pinochle?' I was the only one that raised my hand. Then he asked me where I was from. When I said 'from South Dakota', he said, 'Good, you are coming with me.'

That is how I became a part of the 26th. I was assigned to the 3rd platoon and Sgt. Judson Taylor was my platoon sergeant. He ended up training me to work with the dogs. Ave was the dog I was assigned to. I was in Korea for 14 months and pulled a lot of patrols in the DMZ with Ave. After Sgt. Taylor left, Keith Hermanson was my Sgt."

Dale Thompson and Ave at the Imjim River
Photo from Dale Thompson

Another man, Jack Bransford, tells how another accident played a role in his arrival with the 26th. "I enlisted on February 4th, 1953 in Los Angeles, CA for a three year tour in the US Army. I finished the 16 week infantry light weapons training at Ft. Ord, CA; thereafter I took the 12 week scout dog handler training course at the Army Dog Training Center in Camp Carson with the 40th ISDP. After completion of the training at Camp Carson, while on leave in San Diego, CA, prior to being shipped to Korea with the 40th, I was injured in an accident. When I returned to Camp Carson, I was informed I had been transferred to the 41st ISDP, and given a different dog. My new dog's name was Pal; I was told that the Platoon Leader of the 40th ISDP took my old dog to be his own.

After the 41st completed training, we left by train for Oakland, CA, where subsequently we boarded the USS General R. L Howze and departed for Yokohama, Japan on 1-20-54; we arrived there on 2-4-54. We left the ship on 2-5-54 for Camp Drake, arriving there at 1530 hrs. Lt. Brewster was our Platoon Leader, and SFC Sid Nason was the Platoon Sgt. The personnel of the 41st were advised they were being sent to Hokkaido, Japan. In a surprise announcement, we were informed that five members of the 41st, and their dogs, were being transferred to the 26th ISDP; which was located in Korea with the 2nd Inf. Division. I was notified I was to be one of the 'five,' and informed that my dog Pal would stay with the 41st. He was to be assigned to some guy named 'Anderson', and I was given 'Bruno', Anderson's old dog." The Lucky Five who got pulled to serve with the 26th were Bert Thompson & Clipper, Bill McKendrick & Val, Lloyd Leavitt & a dog whose name no one can recall, Melvin Sexton and Ike, and Jack Bransford and Bruno.

Bill McKendrick and Val at Camp Carson
US Army Photo by Mr. H.L.Stoddard (National Archives)

"Early on the morning of 2-8-54 we left Japan by military air for the K-16 Air Base in Seoul, Korea, where we arrived at 0900 hrs. Later that day the five of us were transported by truck to the 26th ISDP. The 26th was assigned at that time to the Headquarters Company of the 2nd Division; and, we ate our rations at their mess hall. The five of us were then distributed within the three squads of the 26th; Melvin Sexton and I were assigned to the 3rd squad. During the remaining months of my stay in Korea (Feb. 8th to late-November 1954) we functioned as scout dog handlers, and conducted nighttime patrols along the DMZ to detect/deter infiltrators, and to prevent unauthorized intrusions into US Army supply facilities. When on patrol our dog handlers were always armed with loaded weapons, typically a .45 cal. semi-auto pistol and/or a .30 cal. M-2 carbine."

Melvin Sexton and Ike at the swimming hole
Photo from Melvin Sexton

While the 26th was at 2nd Division Headquarters, the scout dog York was again a feature story in Stars and Stripes. The article states "Eighty-five pounds of war dog told it to the IG Friday –springing into his lap in a friendly fashion to state his case. York, a German shepherd of the 26th Scout Dog Plat., was visiting division headquarters with a member of the outfit. Decked out in his Infantry-blue dog blanket with Indianhead patches, York broke loose from his trainer. With a bound he was in the IG office. Another leap landed him in the lap of astonished 1st Lt. Lanford Blangon, Frederick, Oklahoma. Blanton recovered his composure to ask: 'And what's your trouble, soldier?'" (Stars and Stripes, 7-20-1954)

On June 7th, 1954 the 26th re-located to a Signal Corp unit. Although no one remembers the date, our next assignment was to the Headquarters Co. of the 1st Marine Division, located north of the Imjin River; and, this was the final unit with which we served while in Korea. This was the first time since WWII that the Marines utilized scout dogs on patrols. 1st Lt. John B. Carter was the commander of the 25 dogs and handlers.

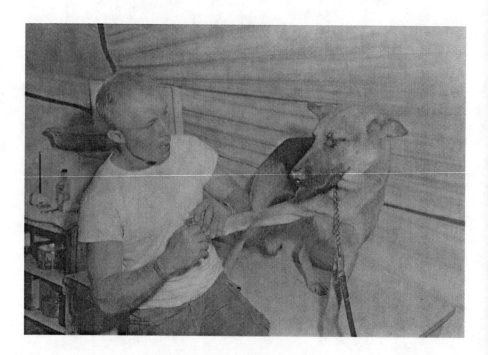

John Drives gives Ajax his pedicure
Photo from John Drives

Jack Bransford tells about how he was able to control his dog by means of subtle commands that were both non-verbal and unconventional. One of these commands was just to squint at someone. "Vetter was the fourth dog that was assigned to me while I was in the army. When I was first assigned to the 26th, Vetter was handled by Cpl Farrand Hall, and was reported to be an experienced scout dog; however, he had a well-earned reputation as a 'biter'. Vetter and Farrand were also assigned to the 3rd squad, so I was well acquainted with them. When Farrand 'rotated' back to the States, Vetter was assigned to me. Initially we experienced some difficulty in establishing a relationship of mutual respect. However, Vetter was the one dog that sticks out in my memory. He was the one I've always remembered, and missed the most when I had to give him up. I connected with him to a greater extent than with any dog before or since. He had a unique and distinct personality. He was very protective of me, and he was an excellent scout dog, with exceptional senses of smell, hearing, and sight – especially at night. Where other dogs were very easy to 'read' when they 'alerted', Vetter's reactions while on patrol were usually very subtle. However, I trusted his alerts, and he was seldom wrong. He was never very friendly with other dogs or people. Vetter had a 'knack' for evidencing signs of friendliness that caused people to doubt me and fail to take my advice—when I admonished them to stay out of his reach to avoid painful consequences—at least, not until after it was too late, and he had grabbed them. There was just such an event that occurred on the boat that transported us from Inchon, Korea to Yokohama, Japan. The event was witnessed by several of my fellow dog-handlers, and involved an Officer who required some needle-work afterwards; fortunately he acknowledged that what resulted was his fault.

Vetter was an exceptional dog; and, he was very intelligent. Much of what I'll describe in the following wasn't unique to Vetter and myself, it was present with the other handlers and their dogs to varying degrees. All of our dogs were obedience trained to respond to both voice and hand commands. The handlers were all trained to observe/study our dogs (which we referred to as 'reading') to note their reaction to certain circumstances or stimulus (which we referred to as an 'alert'). In short, I noticed that frequently Vetter was 'reading' me as much, or more, than I was reading him; and, he was reacting to his analysis of a wide range of situational stimuli. Other handlers experienced the same sort of reaction from their dogs, but more often than not, it only related to simple things, like when the dog was to be fed, or it was apparent they were be taken from their kennel area, or when they could see that their choke chain was about to be replaced with their work-harness. They then reacted in an obvious and predictable manner. Vetter also evidenced these reactions, and many more. As I previously noted, Vetter was very protective of me. When I was present, he always evidenced a high level of situational awareness as to my demeanor and physical movements. If I evidenced signs of stress or agitation, he would reflect an obvious readiness to attack. In fact, if not 'controlled', he would attack. When I first noticed this reactive tendency on his part, the accidental stimulus that I, or another person, had unwittingly provided to trigger the reaction was very obvious. Usually the stimulus was something Vetter 'read' as a threat to me. Upon realizing this, I progressively trained him to react to less and less obvious stimulus from me. For instance, I started by the use of exaggerated jerky motions, and then abruptly looking in a direction that Vetter wasn't looking, to feint that I was startled and in fear, which would activate a 'readiness to attack' response reaction—for which I praised him. I would then 'whoa him' to keep him from trying to attack whatever person was closest. After awhile he became conditioned to that sequence, and would only attack on a command from me, or movement from the person upon whom he was focused. In this situation he would respond to any one of several kinds of stimulus. Thereafter I simply lessened the obviousness of the stimulus I employed to trigger Vetter's protective response—and then praised him. After awhile, I could trigger Vetter's response with virtually no discernible signal from me. This is where the 'eye-squint' came in—it was one of signals I used (if he was looking at me) to trigger his attack response if the person moved, etc. I only did this sort of thing under certain circumstances—because Vetter could and would do a lot of damage to whomsoever, if I didn't control him. To my knowledge, at that time, only Bert Thompson and Williard Peters were fully cognizant of what I just explained." This dog, Vetter, is the same one who saved a whole patrol from being captured or killed by the Chinese earlier in this book.

Williard Peters and Jack Bransford
(Photo from Melvin Sexton)

In late Nov. 1954, all personnel and dogs of the 26th were sent from the assignment with the 1st Marine Division in Korea to the Tokyo Ordnance Depot in Japan. We were informed that our dogs, along with others from various scout dog units, were to be re-trained for sentry dog duty. The men that were previously dog-handlers were given new assignments, or sent stateside for discharge.

Training Area at Tokyo Ordnance Depot
Photo from John Drives

Here we once again meet up with SFC Sidney Nason who was a dog handler with the 26th in Korea in early 1952. He supervised the sentry dogs and their handlers at Tokyo. SFC Nason was happy to see the men and dogs of the 26th. One of the dogs he was reunited with was "Jack". Nason had been on a routine mission on January 3, 1953 with a patrol of 23 men. They encountered a fire fight with the Chinese communists. Evidently Jack's handler was killed or injured in the ensuing skirmish, for he was loose and ran over to Nason's scout dog. Nason immediately captured the dog and returned with him to headquarters when they completed the mission. The dog had straps on his back and was probably a pack animal. He responded well to Chinese commands. Sidney Nason decided that since he was a large German Shepherd and seemed to be quite intelligent, he would re-train him as a scout dog. The dog learned quickly and the two formed a friendship. The dog was named Jack because he was found on a hill called "Jackson Heights" in the Kumwha valley of Korea. In July of 1953, Nason was involved in a battle in

"No Man's Land" for which he received the Distinguished Service Medal. He said that 50 people got shot up that night. He ended up back in the United States. Meanwhile, Jack was assigned to Sgt. Charles Hartnell of Border, Minn. Sgt. Hartnell said the dog handled as well as any dog in the unit. In February, Sid was transferred to the 41st ISDP and chose to accompany them to Japan in late fall of 1954. This is how he ended up in just the right place to see his old war dog, Jack.

SFC Sidney Nason and Jack
Photo from John Drives

Sid says that the commanding officer at Tokyo Ordnance Depot was John R. Phillips. The Japanese were happy to have the war dogs and treated them like gold. They had 50 handlers there and the dogs had a good home. They would be out there before daylight taking care of their dogs. They began with basic obedience training. Then they were agitated and taught to attack. The dogs became very efficient sentry dogs and guarded vast ordnance areas. It was very difficult for Nason to see these wonderful scout dogs taught to be vicious. He felt it was a waste of their capabilities and he chose to move on to another assignment.

Sgt. Tagami, K-9 Commander Mr. Imagami, and Mr. Smokuni
of Tokyo Ordnance Depot
Photo from John Drives

In January, a Cpl Waldrop and Jack Bransford were assigned to establish two more sentry dog units: Cpl Waldrop at the Fuchu Ordnance Depot with 15 – 18 dogs; and Jack Bransford at the Tokorozawa Ordnance Depot with 26 dogs. Jack goes on to say "I reported to the base Security Officer, who was a Lt. Col. (whose name I don't recall). The dog handlers, although untrained for sentry dog work, were Japanese Nationals that were rated at the Black Belt level in martial arts. (In short, they took the job seriously.) There were two handlers for each dog; with a support staff of three, for a total complement of fifty-five personnel. I continued to serve as the NCOIC until approximately August of 1955. Then I was sent to Camp Carson, CO to serve as cadre to train US Air Force personnel as sentry dog handlers – until Feb. 1956 when I was discharged."

Boysan, a trainee, and Duke
Photo from John Drives

Teddy and a Japanese guard in training
Picture from John Drives

Most of the dogs were successfully retrained as sentries. The final disposition of the remaining dogs is unknown; but we are not aware of any dogs, that were 'officially' designated as culls; and none were euthanized as culls. We know that two of these later dogs died. Ron Huber's dog "Rudy" died while still with the Headquarters Co. of the 2nd Division. Rudy was a small dog but he was tough. He was an "agitator" with the other dogs. Sgt. Bowers also had a dog, Major, that died of a brain tumor. He went on to handle Bruno. At least our dogs were not abandoned or euthanized like the war dogs in Vietnam. Ours were a little more fortunate. We couldn't bring them home even though we would have liked to. Most of us wrote letters, asked commanding officers, basically begged everyone we could think of to let us keep our dogs or at least adopt them when they were no longer useful to the military, but to no avail.

Ron Huber and Rudy
Photo from Ron Huber

As far as we know, only two dogs made it home, York and Rommel.
Rommel was the mascot smuggled aboard ship from Korea to Japan by Bill
McKendrick, and then from Japan to the United States by Melvin Sexton.
Melvin says that in Japan, Rommel hung around with the war dogs when

Melvin had patrol duty but he took him for walks whenever he could. When it came time to rotate back to the United States, Melvin went down to a carpenter in town and had him build a big wooden box with a false top compartment. The dog fit into the bottom but if someone opened the lid, they just saw the top contents. Melvin filled the top with the stuff he bought in Japan: souvenirs, jewelry and 4 yards of silk brocade. He was able to get it on board the ship with all the other luggage and men. On the way home, he spent a lot of time on the deck taking care of the dog. A lot of people talked to him but he thinks his 26th Infantry Scout Dog Platoon uniform kept people from asking too many questions. Jack Bransford thinks the people "were just kind enough to look the other way' but in any event, they make the trip safely. When they arrived in the US, the deck hands unloading the ship asked Melvin what they should do with the box. Fortunately, Melvin could see his parents on the dock so he told them to just set it on the dock. They hoisted it down and Melvin's mom took one handle, his dad took the other side, and they just walked off with it–bypassing customs. Melvin exited the ship in the usual manner and Rommel was able to live out his life as a member of the family.

Rommel relaxes with his family
Photo from Melvin Sexton

York was still stationed at Tokyo Ordnance Depot when he reached 8 years old and began to develop rheumatism. The Army had little use for him and issued an order that he be destroyed. But William Welch, an Army Specialist who was an MP and had worked with many dogs on sentry duty, just could not understand why the old hero should be treated that way. "'It seemed wrong to me to destroy a dog that good. I considered the fact that Sergeant York had served the Army so faithfully for eight years, it just wasn't right.' So, the 21 year-old wrote a letter to the Army's Dog Training Center at Fort Carson, Colorado, asking them to reconsider the order. Fort Carson wrote back to Japan, granting a reprieve" for York. (The Independent, 7-3-1956.) York had pulled 148 patrols just between June of 1951 and January of

1953. He continued to lead patrols until the war ended in July of 1953 and then helped patrol the DMZ until the unit was deactivated in November of 1954. He apparently was performing sentry duty until the Army decided he was too old in early 1956. There is no way to tally his total number of patrols. He and Specialist Welch flew home to Travis Air Force Base. York was the first dog in Air Force history to travel as a passenger aboard a Military Air Transport Service flight. Then they traveled to Fort Carson where York was used for publicity and demonstrations.

The Fortunate Dog, York
Photo from John Drives

When the Army Dog Training Center at Fort Carson was inactivated in July 1957, the 26th transferred to Fort Benning, Georgia and York was with them. He had the run of the kennel area and was not confined to his run. As he got older, his hearing and vision began to get worse. He apparently went under a parked truck one day and the driver ran over him. He was transported to the Veterinary Hospital and pronounced dead on arrival. The driver wrote out a report telling what happened and York was buried at Fort Benning. 1st Lt. Thomas J. O'Brien, commanding officer of the unit, wrote a letter to the Commanding General of Fort Benning which details the events. "Army Scout Dog York—Preston Brand Number 011X—was accidentally run over and killed at approximately 0830 hours on 13 August, 1958. York was approximately twelve and one-half years of age. His status while in this unit continued as that of an honored retired member of the platoon." (O'Brien, Thomas J. 25 August, 1958) Unfortunately, when we visited there, we were unable to find anyone who knew the exact site of his burial. It is not marked. York's former handlers were happy to learn that he had a great retirement and died doing what he loved – being part of the action.

During the Korean War, the 26th participated in over 1500 combat patrols. Between June of 1951 and the end of the war on July 27, 1953, they were never put in reserve. They gave support to almost every United States Division and went on patrols with many United Nations Units. The members were awarded a total of three Silver Stars, six Bronze Stars for Valor, and 35 Bronze Stars for meritorious service. Too many of them earned Purple Hearts. They were honored by four Republic of Korea Presidential Unit Citations and the Eighth United States Army gave them a Meritorious Unit Commendation. In part it states: "Throughout its long period of difficult and hazardous service, the 26th Infantry Scout Dog Platoon has never once failed those with whom it served, has consistently shown outstanding devotion to duty in the performance of all of its other duties, and has won on the battlefield a degree of respect and admiration which has established it as a unit of the greatest importance to the Eighth Army. The outstanding performance of duty, proficiency and esprit de corps invariably exhibited by the personnel of this platoon reflect the greatest credit upon themselves and the military service of the United States." (General Orders 114, January 16, 1953 See Appendix A)

When I was over there, I was concerned about the group I was to look out for, and taking care of myself and Hasso. I wasn't focused on the big picture. But after the war, I found out from several different sources that our unit in Korea had cut the casualty rate of ambush and reconnaissance patrols by 60-65%. It feels like we accomplished something, and that is a good feeling. There's a lot of guys who are alive because of the men and dogs of the 26th Infantry Scout Dog Platoon.

Bill McKendrick was able to rescue the 26th guidon before he left Korea
(Photo compliments of Bill McKendrick)

Appendix A: Tribute

STATEMENT OF SERVICE--26TH INFANTRY PLATOON
Constituted March 27, 1944 in the Army as the 26th Quartermaster
War Dog Platoon.

Activated April 1, 1944 at San Carlos, Ca.

Reorganized and redesignated Feb. 3, 1945 as the 26th Infantry
Scout Dog Platoon.

Inactivated Feb. 16, 1946 at Fort Lawton, Washington.

Activated Aug. 1, 1946 at Fort Riley, Kansas.

Allotted April 23, 1951 to the Regular Army

Inactivated Nov. 17, 1954 in Korea

Activated June 15, 1955 at Fort Benning, Georgia

Reorganized and redesignated Nov. 22, 1960 as the 26th Infantry
Platoon (Scout Dog)

Inactivated Nov. 24, 1972 at Fort Benning, Georgia

Withdrawn March 1, 1974 from the Regular Army and allotted to the
Army Reserve; concurrently activated at Pratt, Kansas, as the 26th
Infantry Platoon (Pathfinder/Airborne)

Location changed Sept. 1, 1976 to Wichita, Kansas
Inactivated Sept. 17, 1990 at Wichita, Kansas.

CAMPAIGN PARTICIPATION CREDIT
WORLD WAS II

New Guinea
Luzon (with assault landing-headquarters only)

KOREAN WAR

CCF spring offensive-detachment only
UN summer-fall offensive-detachment only
Second Korean winter
Korea, summer-fall 1952
Third Korean winter
Korea, summer 1953

DECORATIONS

Meritorious Unit Commendation for service in Korea

Philippine Presidential Unit Citation for participation in the war
against the Japanese Empire during the period Oct. 17, 1944 to July 4,
1945.

Four Republic of Korea Presidential Unit Citations for service in Korea.

GENERAL ORDERS   18 January 1953
NUMBER   114

AWARD OF THE MERITORIOUS UNIT COMMENDATION

By direction of the Secretary of the Army, under the provisions of AR 220-315, the Meritorious Unit Commendation is awarded to the following unit of the United States Army for exceptionally meritorious conduct in the performance of outstanding service during the period indicated:

The 26TH INFANTRY SCOUT DOG PLATOON is cited for exceptionally meritorious conduct in the performance of outstanding services in direct support of combat operations in Korea during the period 12 June 1951 to 15 January 1953. The 26TH INFANTRY SCOUT DOG PLATOON, during its service in Korea, has participated in hundreds of combat patrol actions by supporting the patrols with the services of an expert scout dog handler and his highly trained scout dog. The members of the 26TH INFANTRY SCOUT DOG PLATOON, while participating in these patrols, were invariably located at the most vulnerable points in the patrol formation in order that the special aptitudes of the trained dog could be most advantageously used to give warning of the presence of the enemy. The unbroken record of faithful and gallant performance of these missions by the individual handlers and their dogs in support of patrols has saved countless casualties through giving early warning to the friendly patrol of threats to its security. The full value of the services rendered by the 26TH INFANTRY SCOUT DOG PLATOON is nowhere better understood and more highly recognized than amongst the members of the patrols with whom the scout dog handlers and their dogs have operated. When not committed to action, the soldiers of the 26TH INFANTRY SCOUT DOG PLATOON have given unfailing effort to further developing their personal skills as well as that of their dogs in order to better perform the rigorous duties which are required of them while on patrol. Throughout its long period of difficult and hazardous service, the 26TH INFANTRY SCOUT DOG PLATOON has never once failed those with whom it served, has consistently showed outstanding devotion to duty in the performance of all of its other duties, and has won on the battlefield a degree of respect and admiration which has established it as a unit of the greatest importance to the Eighth Army. The outstanding performance of duty, proficiency and esprit de corps invariably exhibited by the personnel of this platoon reflect the greatest credit upon themselves and the military service of the United States.

KAG-PD 200.6

BY COMMAND OF GENERAL VAN FLEET:

OFFICIAL:

B. T. Schantz

B. T. SCHANTZ
Colonel, AGC
Adjutant General

PAUL D. ADAMS
Major General, General Staff
Chief of Staff

Since War Dogs have not been allowed to wear medals since WWII, three of the scout dogs in the 26ᵗʰ were given an Award for Distinguished Service from Major General Samuel T. Williams, of the 25ᵗʰ Infantry Division.

Major General Williams presents David Hull the citation for his dog, "Flash"
US Army Photo by William Jones (National Archives)

25th

INFANTRY   DIVISION

AWARD

FOR

DISTINGUISHED SERVICE

BY THIS INSTRUMENT THE 25th INFANTRY
DIVISION TAKES GRATEFUL COGNIZANCE OF
THE FAITHFUL AND DISTINGUISHED SERVICE
RENDERED IN COMBAT IN KOREA BY U.S. WAR DOG

FLASH

A MEMBER OF THE 26th INFANTRY SCOUT
DOG PLATOON WHO PERFORMED 108 COMBAT
PATROLS BETWEEN 12 JUNE 1951 & 26 JAN 1953

SAMUEL T. WILLIAMS
MAJOR GENERAL USA
COMMANDING

Scout Dog Gray and his Handler PFC Jack Wheeler
US Army Photo by PFC William Jones (US Army Archives)

25th

INFANTRY   DIVISION

AWARD
FOR
DISTINGUISHED SERVICE

BY THIS INSTRUMENT THE 25th INFANTRY
DIVISION TAKES GRATEFUL COGNIZANCE OF
THE FAITHFUL AND DISTINGUISHED SERVICE
RENDERED IN COMBAT IN KOREA BY U.S. WAR DOG

GRAY
PB 0 33 X

A MEMBER OF THE 26th INFANTRY SCOUT
DOG PLATOON WHO PERFORMED 132 COMBAT
PATROLS BETWEEN 12 JUNE 1951 & 26 JAN 1953

SAMUEL T. WILLIAMS
MAJOR GENERAL U.S.A.
COMMANDING

James Partain and York, after receiving citation
US Army Photo by PFC William Jones (National Archives)

25th
INFANTRY DIVISION

AWARD
FOR
DISTINGUISHED SERVICE

BY THIS INSTRUMENT THE 25th INFANTRY
DIVISION TAKES GRATEFUL COGNIZANCE OF
THE FAITHFUL AND DISTINGUISHED SERVICE
RENDERED IN COMBAT IN KOREA BY U.S. WAR DOG

YORK
P B 011 X

A MEMBER OF THE 26th INFANTRY SCOUT
DOG PLATOON WHO PERFORMED 148 COMBAT
PATROLS BETWEEN 12 JUNE 1951 & 26 JAN 1953

SAMUEL T. WILLIAMS
MAJOR GENERAL USA
COMMANDING

May 25, 1997

Mr. Robert E. Fickbohm
RR1, Box 119
Newell, SD 57760

Dear Mr. Fickbohm:

Thank your for your letter of May 19. I enjoyed
hearing from you and learning more about the 26th
Infantry Scout Dog Platoon.

Your daughter and I have been in email contact, in
the course of which she has given me some pointers on
how to locate email addresses. I was astonished that
she found mine; I had never been able to do it, myself.

The scout dogs were a real godsend to us in the 3d
Infantry Division. I was the 3d Division AC/S, G2, from
January, 1953, until I left for home in September of
that year. As G2, I was in charge of patrolling, and
there is no doubt in my mind that the dogs saved many
soldiers' lives. We were able to keep no-man's-land
safe by using three man patrols, each with a dog.
Unfortunately, a new division commander later adopted a
policy of sending out heavy combat patrols, with steel
helmets, heavy weapons, and no dogs. The casualty rate
reflected that mistake, in my opinion.

You have done a great job in reassembling the
members of the dog platoon; 93 is a lot of former
members. Congratulations.

I would enjoy hearing the news of the platoon from
time to time, but I am reluctant to become a member of
any organization to which I can't contribute. Though I
am now 75 years old, I stay mighty busy writing books
on military subjects.

Best of luck in your efforts to reassemble the
26th. And please give my thanks to your daughter.

Sincerely,

John Eisenhower

John S.D. Eisenhower and one of our 26th Dogs

Roster of 26ᵗʰ Who Originally Went to WWII

HEADQUARTERS
WAR DOG RECEPTION AND TRAINING CENTER
SAN CARLOS, CALIFORNIA.

12 May 1944.

SPECIAL ORDERS)
                :
NUMBER   73)   E X T R A C T

      1. Following extract is furnished in accordance with Section IV, WD Circular No. 414 of 1942:

      a.   OFFICERS
           1st Lt. JAMES S. HEAD, 01584340, Commanding

ENLISTED MEN:

T/Sgt	Robertson, Robert K	19083912	T/5	Goucher, Arthur E	33601994
Sgt	Lush, Aubrey S	31027635	T/5	Jackson, William H B	34375736
Sgt	Ormson, Glenn C	36252995	T/5	Long, Leroy	38142172
Sgt	Schut, Herman J.	39682363	T/5	Murphy, Richard	36825866
T/5	Aldred, Russell E	37701899	T/5	Oliver, Frank	36585717
T/5	Bertram, George P	37349804	T/5	Skillings, Walter W	31383619
T/5	Biancucci, Paul J	31344145	T/5	Smith, Edwin P	35705071
T/5	Blackmon, Benjamin T	38512966	T/5	Thompson, Russell	39377423
T/5	Cohen, Burton I	31378926	T/5	Tucker, Ellis A	31378642
T/5	Cranford, Robert D	38515857	T/5	Valenzuela, Carlos O	39690978
T/5	Davidson, Harold K	15132916	T/5	Williams, David M	37673501
T/5	Diller, George E	33700484	Pvt	Leavitt, Milton A	31364439
T/5	Di Pilla, Leonida A	31051038	Pvt	Smith, Ray H	38507403
T/5	Garbo, William	34637457	Pvt	Sullivan, Jack N	39001014
T/5	Gatto, Giovanni C.	31383836			

      b. War Dog Reception and Training Center, San Carlos, Calif.

      c. On or about 14 May 1944 - Motor.

      d. San Francisco (Fort Mason), Calif.

TDN. TOWFN Motor transpn. 1-5000 P 431-02 A 0425-24. Auth: Conf ltr Hq Ninth Service Command, Ft Douglas Utah, 17 April 1944, File 370.5 (SPRSA), subject: Movement Orders, and VOCG SFPOE, 11 May 1944.

    *   *   *   *   *   *   *   *

      By Order of Colonel KOESTER:

                            CHESTER A. SNYDER, JR
                            1st Lt., Q.M.C.
                            Adjutant

OFFICIAL:

Chester A. Snyder Jr.
CHESTER A. SNYDER, JR
1st Lt., Q.M.C.
Adjutant

Roster of WWII 26th Going to Japan

PASSENGER LISTS AND ROSTERS

PASSENGER LIST

1st Class; Second; Troop.   LST 909   23 September 1945

From: Luzon, P.I.   To:

NO.	NAME	RANK	SERIAL NO.	REMARKS

PLATOON ROSTER

26th INFANTRY SCOUT DOG PLATOON

(1st Lt. Head, James S.   01584340)
(2d Lt.   Steinhoff, Homer E.01597629)

NO.	NAME	RANK	SERIAL NO.
1.	Biancucci, Paul J.	T/Sgt	31344145
2.	Edwards, Harvey D.	Sgt	34328748
3.	Oliver, Frank	Sgt	36585717
4.	Schut, Herman J.	Sgt	39682363
5.	Sullivan, Jack N.	Sgt	39001014
6.	Williams, David M.	Sgt	37673501
7.	Marcinkiewicz, Alphonse	T/4	32346054
8.	Moore, Sonny E.	Cpl	39416201
9.	Bertram, George P.	T/5	37349804
10.	Cohen, Burton I.	T/5	31378926
11.	Cranford, Robert D.	T/5	38515857
12.	Di Pilla, Leonida A.	T/5	31053038
13.	Gatto, Giovanni C.	T/5	31383836
14.	Gibson, James	T/5	35706131
15.	Pykiet, Alvin B.	T/5	37751852
16.	Smith, Edwin P.	T/5	35705871
17.	Smith, Ernest J.	T/5	36048864
18.	Tucker, Ellis A.	T/5	31378642

Roster of 26th at End of War or not on Either of Prior Rosters

Crenshaw, James E.   DuQuette, Leo R.
Layher, William S.   Nelson, Ralph D.
Coates, Robert C.   Ferrell, Leonard
Raye, Edwin L.

Partial Roster of Those Who Served In 26ᵗʰ During Korean War Era
(There may have been others whose names weren't remembered or were not on
rosters—many personnel records were burned in fire)

Experimental Group: Assigned to 3ʳᵈ Reconnaissance Company on
6-12-1951
Irving, Cpl. William J, commander, dog-Jon

Bristol, Robert, dog-Hamlet   Green, Huda.L, dog-Berry
Pollard, Larry B, dog-Orrin   Potts, Robert M , dog-York
Price,Virgil E, dog-Leo   Rose, Farnia, dog-Pen

Replacements:
Butler, Howard A   Fahey, Edward M
Grossman, Robert A.   Hoover, William
Nix, Dale

1st Group:
1ˢᵗ squad: attached to 2ⁿᵈ Infantry Division
Claus, Carl   Deaner, Bert
Heffron, James   North, Jack
Stipe, Hazen   Strawder, Kenneth
Trickey, Ralph   Ward, Harry

2ⁿᵈ squad: attached to 40ᵗʰ Infantry
Armstrong, Charles   Bushnell, Bruce
Haak, Clayton   Kraun, Fred
McKeown, Ron   Meyers, Max
Patterson, Robert

1ˢᵗ group that didn't go to Korea:
Dean, John   Hibbard, William
Ishimoto, Kenneth   Jones, Norman
McMahon, Lewis   Norgoard, Alou
Norwood, Patrick   Rogen, Alton
Thayer, Roy   Thrift, Herbert
Willoughby, Jack

1st Group Replacements
Anderson , Orville   Bollschweiler, Robert
Booth, Reinhart   Brezwell, Joe
Burke, Cornelius   Clawson, James
Delille, Robert   Kobin, John

Piatt, Larry
Wheeler, Jack

Stahl, Donald

2rd Group

Brice, Victor
Covington, Percy
Haines, Robert
Hoindl, James
Horn, Myron
Hunt, Charles
Klenz, James
Kunberger, James
Mitchell, Ted
Partain, James
Ross, Leroy C.
Smith, Don
Steeneck, Alvin
Thompson, Joseph
Westphal, Frederick
Wommack, James

Coleman, Lloyd
Goodwin, Robert
Hamp, Conrad
Holt, Billy R.
Hull, David
Johnston, James W.
Kornder, Roger
Little, Philip
Nason, Sid
Robinson, Dale
Serio, Andrew
Smith, Keith
Sylvestor, Ramon
Treeece, Clyde
Willis, Robert G.

3rd Group

Cheatwood. James
Eversole, Shafter
Hartnell, Charles
McFarland, Merle
O'Connell, Leroy
Suiter, Leo

Clifton, John
Fickbohm, Robert
Hermanson, Keith
Morning, William
Taylor, Jud

3rd Group Replacements

Bowers, Julian
Maupin, BJ
Thompson, Dale

Gittleson, Larry
Shipman, Norman
Walker, William

4th Group

Bane, Virgil
Blix, Marshall
Drives, John
Gaghan, Lawrence
Gose, Billy
Hillier, Carl
Huber, Ronald

Berger, Ballard
Bransford, Jack
Findley, Nelson
Garner, Richard
Hall, Farrand
Heintzelman, Richard
Hunt, Fred

Hunt, Jack
Hunt, Norman
Kinney, James
Leavitt, Lloyd E.
McKendrick, William
Peters, Williard
Rickels, Rex
Secrist, Donald
Thompson, Bert
Wessels, Harlan

Hunt, John E.
Jarrett, Hiawatha
Kirk, William E.
McDonald, Willie
Moscatello, Oresto
Phillips, Roger J.
Scarborough, Alvin
Sexton, Melvin
Walker, Richard
Wetherington, William

Partial Roster of Dogs Who Served in Korea
(strictly from men's memories, cannot find official records)

AJAX	ARLO
AVE	BARRON
BARRY	BLACK KING
BLACK TIM	BLITZ
BRUNO	BUCK
CAPPY	CHAMP (KIA)
CHARLEY (KIA)	DUFFY
DUKE	ETU
FLASH	FOX
FRITZ	GRAY
HAMLET	HAPPY (KIA)
HANS	HASSO
HAVOC	IKE
JACK	JIGGER
JON	LANCE
LEO (KIA)	KING
KING III	KING IV
KING #5	LADDIE
MAJOR	MEEGON
ORRIN	PAL
PENDENES	PEN
PILOT	PRINCE
REX (KIA)	RICKEY
ROGGIE	RUDY
RUSTY	SHEBA
STARK	STONEY
TEDDY	THOR
TIM	TIM II
TONY	TRISTUM
VAL	VETTER
WOLF	YORK

Appendix B: Group Photos

Photograph taken of my WWII graduation class not all of whom ended up with the 26th;
1st Row, down front: left to right: Graves, Stein, Funk. Instructor and Assistants
2nd Row: Gitreau, Davidson, Junker, Gatto, Land, EcKard, Williams A., Darv.
3rd Row: Garbo, _____, _____, Riordan, Griffith, Sattler, DiChara, _____, Eberhart.
4th Row: Skillings, Hochban, Williams T., Andrews, Nolan, Brenning, Soloman, Walker.
Photo compliments of Bill Garbo

WWII Dogs Were Given Discharge Certificates, This One Belongs to Captain
Copy From Sonny Moore

Top left to right: Bert Deaner, James Heffron and Hasso, John Kobin and Jigger, Kenneth Strawder and Ave, Charles Armstrong and Prince, Jack Wheeler and Orrin, Hazen Stipe and Flash, William Hoover and Hyper?

Center left to right: Fred Kraun and Rusty, Harry Ward and Grey, Max Meyers and Stark, Bruce Bushnell and Hamlet, Clayton Haak and Wolf, Ronald McKeown and Champ, Edward Fahey and Hans

Bottom left to right Larry Piatt and Charlie, Don Stahl and Happy, Reinhard Booth and Tim, Robert Patterson and York, Joe Brezwell and Tim #2, Jim Clawson (Pen got cut out of the photo)

Photo taken July 15, 1952, compliments of Jack Wheeler

TOP-Robert Goodwin, Clyde Treece, Edward Turner, LeRoy Ross, Ramon Sylvestor
MIDDLE—Myron Horn, Philip Little, Alvin Steeneck, Charles Hartnell, Fred Westphal, Charles Hunt
BOTTOM—Dale Robinson, Shafter Eversole, Jud Taylor, ?, Ted Mitchell, David Hull, Percy Covington
Picture from Jim Cheatwood

Top l-r: Roger Kornder, Edward Hamp, Fed Westphal, Andy Serio, Robert Goodwin, Ramon Sylvestor
Middle: LeRoy O'Connell, John Clifton, William Morning, Dale Robinson, Bob Fickbohm, Keith Hermanson
Bottom: Merle McFarlane, Robert Bollschweiler, Ted Mitchell, Sid Nason, Myron Horn, Robert Willis, Jim Cheatwood
Photo compliments of Robert Fickbohm

Top left to right: Rex Rickels, Lloyd Leavitt, Alvin Scarborough, Ballard Berger, ? behind camera
Bottom: Norman Hunt, Marshall Blix, Bill Gose, Jim Kinney Photo compliments of Harlan Wessels

The 26th Infantry Scout Dog Platoon doing a close order drill march May 6, 1954
US Army Photo by CPL James Welshman, 3rd Signal Co.

Appendix C: Dogs In Present Day

War dogs today are not called "war dogs" but military working dogs. And yes, they are very much alive and well. Military working dogs are now multi-trained. Sentry dogs are trained for attack, drug sniffing and explosives. Scout dogs are still a little better trained as they have to be absolutely silent and specialized.

US Special Ops found information about the 26th on the computer through my daughter, Sandra. They wanted to know if she knew any combat veteran scout dog handlers and she told them she knew quite a few. They said they wanted to know if she could send a combat veteran to a K-9 conference in Fort Brag, NC in February of 2010. They were very happy to hear that she could easily find a Korean War Veteran and knew two WWII veterans that might be able to visit as well. She talked to Bill Garbo and I and we decided to go. There were also four Vietnam dog men, mostly trackers, who also attended. I guess I'm now back working in intelligence so I'm limited as to how much information to share, but I can tell you that the K-9 handlers we met were working with US Army Special Ops. Being invited to speak to them was quite an honor for me. Each of us gave a 50 minute presentation and then there were several opportunities for questions and answers. These soldiers treated us very well, put us up at the Mariott, gave us $50 per diem, and paid all travel expenses. We ate at their mess hall at noon and the food was better than most fancy cafes I've eaten in. They looked out for our every need and treated us with honor and respect. We certainly enjoyed gathering with war dog handlers from WWII through the present war.

Special Ops is an interesting place. It appears that quite a number of them have done a hitch or two, and are now working as civilians for the army. There was a big, black dog who had the run of the K-9 conference. He had a beautiful disposition. He is a recovered WIA and a discharged veteran who is the constant companion of his handler and master. He took a bullet through the chest. He is recovered now, with not so much as a limp, probably thanks to the unit veterinary technician. They also have a graveyard for those canines who made the ultimate sacrifice and a growing number of markers. I believe they have lost more dogs than the 26th did in 17 months of constant combat. They are developing a memorial and appreciate contributions.

Basic training for the pups and men is being done at Lackland Air Force Base, and Fort Bragg is the finishing school. I've got to say, I was impressed with the K-9 and Special Ops arrangement. I do believe if the 26th would have had the backing of US Special Ops, we would have accomplished more, and done better reconnaissance and ambush patrols. We probably would have captured more POWs. Most likely someone will write a book about this group's history someday, for I'm sure there is history in the making there at Fort Bragg.

When I came back from the conference, I made a prediction that if old Bin Laden was found, there would probably be a military working dog involved. Then we hear in the news that the dog, Cairo, went in with Team Six. That excited a lot of us dog handlers. I was at Pendleton Navy Base last fall when I attended my grandson, Ronald's, graduation from Marine basic training at San Diego. They were training dogs so I told my grandson that if he got bored with fixing helicopters, he could maybe transfer over to dogs for a little excitement.

There is certainly a lot of action yet today for our military working dog handlers and they are doing a fine job of saving lives. There are more than 600 dogs in Iraq and Afghanistan alone. On the very day that we sent this to the publisher, we saw in the news that 30 U.S.soldiers were killed when their helicopter was shot down in Afghanistan. Among them was a dog handler and his military working dog. They all made the ultimate sacrifice for other's freedom. We have many other dogs working alongside our policemen, security guards, and search and rescue teams. They are making airports, military bases, and our streets safer. We hope that this book encourages our readers to appreciate the job that all of these canines have done in the past and are still doing every day.

Sources Cited

Adams, Maj. Gen. Paul D. "Award of the Meritorious Unit Commendation" by Command of General Van Fleet, 8th Army, January 18, 1953

"Airborne Dogs" Stars and Stripes Newspaper, 2/12/1954

"Army Scout Dogs Shown", Centralia Newspaper, Centralia, WA April 24, 1947.

Atchison Daily Globe, Atchison, KS 4/6/1952

Brown, Sgt. Dave, "Squad of War Dogs New on Recon Duty" Stars and Stripes Pacific Edition, 9/4/1951

Boon, Major Kevin, Quartermaster Army Website 1998 *(www.quartermaster. army.mil/oqmg/Professional_Bulleting/1998/Spring_1998/qmk9)*

Bransford, Jack. "My 3 Years in the US Army" email 2/7/2010 and phone conversations to S. Granger

Diller, George. Letters and Interview by S. Granger, Oct. 2009

"Dog Saves 15 Yanks on Korea Front Patrol", Stars and Stripes European Edition, 2/23/53

Downey, Fairfax. Dogs for Defense: American Dogs in the Second World War, 1941-45 by Direction and Authorization of the Trustees Dogs For Defense, Inc. Edited and Distributed by Daniel P. McDonald, New York, NY 1955

Eisenhower, John S.D. letter to R. Fickbohm May 25, 1997

Ferrell, Buck. letter to S. Granger September 2008

Garbo, William, World War II Memoirs (unpublished manuscript, given to S. Granger, copyright 1946) and email Jan. 17, 2009

Green, Cpl. H.L. letter to 26th ISDP, at San Francisco, CA, 12 July, 1951

Gray, Ernest A. Dogs of War, Published by Robert Hale Limited, Great Britain 1989

Haahp,1st Lt. Louis J. Infantry, letter to 26th Quartermaster War Dog Platoon on 26 November 1944

Haak, Clayton. personal account at Sturgis Reunion 1995, letters to S. Granger, and letter to mother, June 1952

Hanna, Walter J., Infantry Commanding Officer, letter dated 22 December, 1944 from the Office of the Regimental Commander

Hartnell, Charles, Interview at 26th Reunion

Head, 1st Lt. James S., Report of 26th QM War dog Plat. July 5, 1944 and Historical Report to Commanding General July 18, 1945 (National Archives)

Heffron, SFC James G. After Action Interview by Briscoe, Major Pierce W., Saemal, Korea, October 29, 1952. Military History Detachment, 8086 AU "The 26th Infantry Scout Dog Platoon, Project No. MHD-5(Fort McNair)

Hoover, William, letter to S. Granger, October 27, 2009

Hunt, Charles. Interview by S.Granger, October 2009

Hymoff, Ed. "Scout Dog Whines Remind Yanks of Buddy's Death on Fatal Mission" Starts and Stripes Pacific Edition, 11/27/1952

Ish, Lt. Col. George. Letter to R. Fickbohm, January 1996

"K-9 Corpsman Tells It to Indianhead IG" Stars and Stripes, S. Korea, 7-20-1954

Lemish, Michael G. War Dogs: A History of Loyalty and Heroism, published by Brassey's Inc. Copyright 1996

Lemnitzer, Maj. Gen. "Operation of Scout Dogs and Dog Handlers on Patrols" Saemal, Korea June 1952. National Archives

Little, Phillip. Personal account to R. Fickbohm, 2008

"Loving a Soldier" Poem – unknown source and author

"Master Has Cot in Hospital Beside Wounded War Dog", Galveston Daily News, Galveston, TX 4/16/1945

McKeown, Ronald. "Nostalgic Remembrances of Ronald A. McKeown", email to S. Granger 2/2008

Miller, Lee G. "War Dogs Can Detect Enemy 800 Yards Away" The Brownsville Herald, Brownsville, TX 6-8-1945

"Mobilization Training Program No. 10-5" War Department, Washington, DC July 1, 1944 (National Archives)

Moore, Sonny, "My Time" account, photos, and documents that he gave R. Fickbohm, Fall 2005

Mortensen, Benjamin F. Diary of a Frontline Chaplain Aspen Books, June 1997.

"Nebraska Army Post Trains All War Dogs", The Nebraska State Journal, June 17, 1945

North, Sgt. Jack. After Action Interview by Major Pierce W. Briscoe, Saemal, Korea, October 30, 1952. Military History Detachment, 8086 AU "The 26th Infantry Scout Dog Platoon, Project No. MHD-5(Fort McNair)

O'Brien, Thomas J. letter to Commanding General of US Army Infantry Center at Fort Benning, Georgia, dated 25 August, 1958

Parks, Howard N. "Tactical Employment of the Infantry Scout Dog" Student monograph, Advanced Infantry Officers Course, 1956. (Military History Institute)

Partain, Jim. Interview with R. Fickbohm in November 2000.

"Platoon Pays Respects to Patrol Dog" Stars and Stripes, Pacific Edition, January 18, 1953

Pfaffenberger, Clarence and Finnegan, George. Paper on War Dog Return Success, National Archives

Prilliman, Richard. Interview taken from "Tactical Employment of the Infantry Scout Dog" by Captain Howard N. Parks, Student Monograph, Advanced Infantry Officers Course ,1956, (Military History Institute)

Sanderson, Jeannette. War Dog Heroes, Published by Scholastic,Inc. April 1997

Sexton, Melvin. Email and phone conversation with S. Granger, July 31, 2011

"Sgt. David Williams War Dog Gives Alert In Enemy's Presence", Carroll Daily Times-Herald, Carroll, Iowa, 8/3/1945

Steeneck, Alvin. personal account to R. Fickbohm, Sept. 1996

Strawder, Ken. phone interview by S. Granger, Oct. 7, 2009

Suiter, 1st Lt. Leo F. letter to Commanding General of 2nd Infantry Division, 8 August 1953 and interview by S.Granger, October 2009

Summers, Harry G. Jr. Korean War Almanac published by Facts on File, April 1991

Thompson, Dale. "My story" email to S. Granger, 11/23/2009

"Trainer Tells of Dog's Heroism on Morotai Island" Southtown Economist, Chicago, IL 1/3/1945

Trickey, Ralph. "My Own History" computer file emailed to his daughter-in-law, Christine Trickey on 11/20/2008 and personal account at Sturgis Reunion 1995

Waller, Anna. "Dogs and National Defense" Report 1958 (National Archives)

"War Dogs Sniff Out 'Red' Meat", Portsmouth Times, Portsmouth, OH 7-6-1951

Wheeler, Jack. "Patrol" email to S. Granger, 10/6/2008

White, Sid. "Dog Hero, GI Fly Home", The Independent, Pasadena, CA 7/3/1956.

Wiley, Bonnie. "America's War Dogs Hound Japanese in South Pacific" The Abilene Reporter-News, Abilene, TX May 7, 1944

"Winburne Sergeant", The Progress, Clearfield, PA April 25, 1947

Zika, Dick. personal account & documents to R. Fickbohm, at CBI Reunion 1996

CPSIA information can be obtained at www.ICGtesting.com
Printed in the USA
LVOW062322220113

316711LV00004B/286/P